Reit

Understanding How to Analyze Reits

(How You Can Develop a New Source of Passive Income in No Time)

Robert Lawlor

Published By **Cathy Nedrow**

Robert Lawlor

Reit: Understanding How to Analyze Reits (How You Can Develop a New Source of Passive Income in No Time)

ISBN 978-1-7773242-8-5

No part of this guidebook shall be reproduced in any form without permission in writing from the publisher except in the case of brief quotations embodied in critical articles or reviews.

Legal & Disclaimer

The information contained in this book is not designed to replace or take the place of any form of medicine or professional medical advice. The information in this book has been provided for educational & entertainment purposes only.

The information contained in this book has been compiled from sources deemed reliable, and it is accurate to the best of the Author's knowledge; however, the Author cannot guarantee its accuracy and validity and cannot be held liable for any errors or omissions. Changes are periodically made to this book. You must consult your doctor or get professional medical advice before using any of the suggested remedies, techniques, or information in this book.

Table Of Contents

Chapter 1: Real Estate Investment Trusts

Mark Twain as quick as said, "Buy land; they'll be no longer making it anymore."

Louis Glickman moreover said, "The tremendous funding on this planet is earth."

Andrew Carnegie, an American Industrialist and one of the wealthiest Americans in information, additionally said, "The smart younger man or salary earner of these days invests his cash in actual property."

All of these realistic guys who've unarguably left their marks on the sands of time allude to the reality that real assets making an investment is one of the wonderful methods to build up wealth and benefit your monetary objectives.

But there's continuously one trouble that hinders most humans from taking advantage of this splendid funding technique- capital.

Not genuinely everyone can give you the cash for hundreds of hundreds to buy a belongings. Even house flipping couldn't come cheap, as you will maximum probably need upwards of $10,000 to shop for a residence, and that doesn't embody the cash you'll need to renovate the property in advance than you could sell it for a income.

But long gone are the instances even as conventional actual assets making an investment come to be the best desire to be had to involved consumers.

These days, there are numerous unique non-conventional techniques to get worried in the real assets market, in spite of minimal capital and whilst no longer having to very own any belongings.

Traditional real property making an investment normally consists of searching for physical homes, which includes unmarried-own family houses, multi-family condominium houses, or commercial houses, and generating income via renting those residences out to tenants or selling them for a profits at the equal time as assets values understand.

However, proudly owning physical belongings moreover comes with vast obligations and dangers. You'll want to maintain the assets, find out tenants, and manage any upkeep or renovation issues that upward thrust up.

Plus, if the real belongings marketplace tales a downturn, you could face financial losses if the price of your own home decreases.

Alternatively, you can spend money on actual property with out buying assets and this is through investments in REITs.

Before we dive into the middle of a manner to put money into REITs, it is critical to recognize some key phrases and thoughts and a few elements that have an impact at the actual property market, as this could be crucial in studying and making investment alternatives.

Supply and Demand

Like some other market, the actual property market is inspired thru deliver and speak to for.

Prices generally tend to growth even as there's a immoderate name for for homes and a confined supply. Conversely, prices will be predisposed to decrease even as there's a low name for for houses and an oversupply.

Location

Properties in perfect places, which embody humans with authentic schools, access to public transportation, and proximity to well-known facilities, have a propensity to have higher values than those in lots a lot much less right places.

Property Value

Understanding how belongings values are determined can assist traders make informed picks approximately their actual estate investments.

A variety of things, which include region, length, state of affairs, and the present day u . S . Of the real assets marketplace determines the fee of a property.

Factors that Affect Property Values

These factors decide the charge of actual property residences. They moreover decide the charge and common performance of the stocks of something REITs you make a decision to put money into.

Interest Rates

Interest expenses have a brilliant impact at the real belongings market. When hobby costs are low, it will become extra low price for human beings to buy houses and invest in actual assets.

This can reason prolonged call for for homes and a corresponding fee increase.

Conversely, at the same time as hobby costs are immoderate, it can deter people from investing in real property, foremost to a decrease in call for and fees.

Economic Conditions

The us of a of the financial tool also can impact the real assets market. When the economic system is robust and unemployment fees are low, humans will be inclined to have more disposable earnings and can be more likely to spend money on actual belongings.

However, at the same time as the financial gadget is susceptible, and unemployment costs are excessive, humans can be a great deal less likely to spend money on real assets, lowering name for and fees.

Demographics

Demographics, which consist of populace increase and age distribution, can also have an effect on the real property market.

For instance, because of the truth the Baby Boomer technology some time and starts offevolved offevolved offevolved to retire, there may be an improved name for for senior residing centers and retirement agencies.

Local Market Conditions

Finally, nearby marketplace situations, which includes zoning legal guidelines, tax expenses, and the provision of land, also can affect the actual property market.

It is critical to realize those neighborhood factors at the same time as making real assets investment choices.

What are Real Estate Investment Trusts?

Real Estate Investment Trusts (REITs) are entities that very own and look over real estate assets that generate income collectively with buying department stores, workplace homes, and home complexes.

They generally invest in a diverse variety of actual property houses at some stage in numerous geographic areas and sectors, that could help spread and limit hazard have to any single belongings or location underperform.

REITs can be public or non-traded. REITs which is probably publicly traded are indexed on a inventory alternate and may be presented and acquired like every other inventory, whilst non-traded REITs should be bought thru a supplier or economic representative as they're no longer traded on a stock exchange market.

REITs are mandated through law to distribute not less than ninety% in their taxable earnings to shareholders in dividends, so as an investor, you're constantly first-rate of a ordinary deliver of passive profits from your investments.

Real Estate Investment Trusts (REITs) are also substantially smooth to put money into and provide liquidity, which means you could buy and promote shares your shares at the stock change market similar to every other publicly traded enterprise.

How REITs Work

Let's say you want to spend money on actual belongings but do now not have the capital or desire to shop for and manage bodily property. Instead, you could decide to put money into a REIT.

So you do your research and discover a publicly listed and traded REIT that owns and operates numerous condominium houses across the u . S ..

The REIT is selling its stocks at $1 consistent with percentage.

Then making a decision to invest $10,000 through looking for $10,000 certainly worth of the REIT's stocks in the stock exchange market.

Over the following one year, the REIT's apartment houses generate $1 million in apartment income. Because, as a shareholder, you're entitled to a part of this earnings within the form of dividends and due to the fact the REIT is wanted to distribute as a minimum 90% of its taxable earnings to shareholders, you bought a dividend charge of $nine,000 ($1 million x 90% / 10,000 stocks).

In addition to producing earnings through dividends, your REIT investment's fee may additionally moreover increase through the years. Let's say the choice for for houses inside the regions wherein the REIT owns properties will boom. In this case, the rate of the REIT's shares can also additionally upward push as nicely, making it feasible in an effort to promote your shares at a profits.

Benefits of Investing In Real Estate Investment Trusts

Investing in Real Estate Investment Trusts can offer an entire lot of advantages for investors, including:

1.   Potential for robust earnings

REITs are required to distribute 90% taxable profits to shareholders within the form of dividends, that could provide a ordinary circulate of earnings for clients.

2.   Investment Portfolio Diversification

Investing in REITs also can assist you diversify your portfolio past stocks and bonds.

3.   Liquidity

REITs are traded on maximum crucial stock exchanges, because of this they will be fantastically liquid and can be bought and offered with out issue.

4.   Professional Management:

REITs are managed with the useful resource of expert real belongings managers with big industry experience who may want to make knowledgeable alternatives concerning belongings investments.

5.   Low Minimum Investment

Investing in REITs requires pretty low minimum investments, making them to be had to a widespread range of consumers.

6. Tax Benefits

REIT dividends are usually taxed at a lower rate than unique varieties of funding profits, that would assist reduce your everyday tax criminal duty as an investor.

7. Exposure to Different Sectors

REITs spend money on quite a few diverse actual belongings sectors, which include residential, enterprise, enterprise, and healthcare, which permits you, as an investor, to diversify your holdings.

eight. Potential for capital appreciation

REITs can provide possibilities for capital appreciation via assets appreciation and rental profits growth.

The Not-So-Pretty Side of Investing in Real Estate Investment Trusts

Investing in Real Estate Investment Trusts (REITs) can offer many blessings, but like a few different funding method, there also are numerous downsides that you have to be aware of in advance than making an investment.

Some functionality downsides of creating an funding in REITs encompass:

1.   Market Volatility

REITs can be pretty risky, and their price can range relying on market situations. This technique you could enjoy large losses at some point of market downturns, that would once in a while be tough to get over.

2.   Interest Rate Sensitivity

REITs are sensitive to hobby prices. Higher interest prices can growth their borrowing fees and in the long run lessen their profitability.

This method that after interest costs upward push, REITs can see a decline in rate.

3.   Inflation Risks

Inflation may additionally furthermore erode the fee of REITs over time, due to the fact the costs of preserving and managing the homes they constitute can boom with out a corresponding growth within the fee of apartment profits.

four.   Management Risks

REITs are controlled by means of way of using experts, and the excellent of the control organization should have a big effect on the overall overall performance of the receive as actual with.

Poor management can reason underperformance and large losses that may impact your profits.

5.   Property-Specific Risks

REITs are uncovered to assets-unique risks that could impact their returns.

REITs personal a portfolio of homes, and the value of these homes can be stricken by a selection of factors, collectively with adjustments in zoning legal guidelines, herbal disasters, or tenant defaults.

6.   Regulatory Risks

Since REITs are situation to rules and tax prison hints, there may be a danger that law changes may moreover need to impact the believe's overall performance.

7.   Concentration Risk

Some REITs specialize in specific forms of houses, together with place of job homes or shopping shops.

This way that in case you put money into a REIT specializing in a specific kind of assets, you're exposed to recognition hazard, which can impact your returns if that market section memories a downturn.

eight. Dividend Risks

REITs are required to pay out as a minimum 90% of their taxable income as dividends to shareholders, which may be attractive to profits-searching out consumers.

However, there's a risk that the REIT may be not able to keep its dividend bills if condominium profits declines or it wants to preserve extra income for preservation or expansion.

9.   Performance Fees

Some REITs fee prevalent performance prices to their managers, which could reduce your commonplace returns as an investor.

10.   Lack of Control

When you spend money on a REIT, you do now not right now very very own the homes that the keep in thoughts owns.

This technique you have got were given limited manage over how the houses are controlled and maintained, that may impact their rate over time.

Types of Real Estate Investment Trusts

There are special types of Real Estate funding trusts, and each one operates in a remarkable and specific manner.

1.   Public Real Estate Investment Trust

Public REITs are indexed on the inventory trade, and their stocks can resultseasily be provided and bought at the stock change market, making them especially liquid.

They are also greater transparent than one of a kind types of REITs due to the fact they will be required via the Securities and Exchange Commission (SEC) to sign on and publicly divulge information about their holdings and sports activities sports, so you, as an investor, may be capable of apprehend what is taking place collectively at the side of your investments usually.

2. Public Non-Traded Real Estate Investment Trust

Public non-listed REITs (PNLRs) also are legally required to be registered with the Securities and Exchange Commission (SEC). They perform in nearly every awesome manner as indexed REITs; but, they do now not alternate on essential inventory exchanges. Also, they're a lot much less liquid than publicly listed REITs as they often face some redemption policies.

For instance, traders may be required to preserve without delay to their stocks for a minimum length earlier than being allowed to sell them off.

Some PNLRS can also have buy-decrease back restrictions because of this that that have to making a decision to promote your stocks, you could handiest promote them over again to the organization.

three. Private Real Estate Investment Trust

Private REITs are not legally required to be registered with the Securities and Exchange Commission (SEC). They also are no longer legally required to expose statistics approximately their investment operations to the general public.

This way as an investor, you can in the essential be saved within the dark about what goes on on the aspect of your investments.

They also are no longer as liquid as publicly traded REITs. Finding other shoppers to shop for the shares off your arms need to you ever need your cash can be an onerous challenge.

However, investment in REIT is simplest available to prevalent shoppers and funding groups. Regular customers are regularly restrained from making an funding in private actual estate investment trusts.

Types of Real Estate Investment Trust Stocks

REIT additionally may be labeled in step with the type or elegance of property that the commercial enterprise organization focuses on:

Equity Real Estate Investment Trusts: Equity REITs gather homes with the sole aim of earning income from renting or leasing those homes to tenants.

They generally spend money on commercially possible homes at the side of administrative center complexes, buying branch stores, hotels, condo complexes, and plenty of others.

Their aim is to earn cash from rent or belongings appreciation.

Mortgage Real Estate Investment Trusts: Mortgage REITs also are referred to as mREITs.

As the decision implies, those are actual assets investment trusts that make coins from interest on real assets loans.

They do not normally personal or manipulate residences. Instead, they provide loan loans to human beings inquisitive about looking for real property, and in trade, they rate hobby on those loans.

The motive is to earn earnings from the difference among funding expenses and interest profits on their mortgage assets.

Hybrid Real Estate Investment Trusts: Hybrid actual assets investment trusts are corporations whose portfolios consist of every equity and loan asset investments.

They make coins from interest on actual belongings mortgage loans, as well as from rental earnings and assets appreciation.

Healthcare Real Estate Investment Trusts: Healthcare actual assets funding trusts (REITs) are a form of REIT that invests in healthcare-themed homes collectively with hospitals, clinical workplace homes, nursing homes, assisted dwelling centers, and one-of-a-type kinds of healthcare centers.

Healthcare REITs generate earnings by means of way of leasing their houses to healthcare providers over an prolonged-time period period. These carriers benefit from the stability and predictability of having an prolonged-term lease, at the identical time due to the fact the REIT blessings from a consistent flow into of condo earnings.

One of the number one advantages of creating an investment in healthcare REITs is that they'll be a bargain less risky than one-of-a-kind styles of actual property investments. This is because of the reality that call for for healthcare offerings is surprisingly solid, even sooner or later of economic downturns.

Furthermore, demographic developments such as an getting old populace and multiplied call for for healthcare services may benefit healthcare REITs.

As the Baby Boomer era a while, there may be extra call for for healthcare centers along with nursing homes and assisted living facilities, which may also additionally moreover electricity up the income and profitability potentials for healthcare REITs.

Healthcare REITs can be a valuable addition to a assorted actual assets investment portfolio as they are capable of offer constant earnings, strong returns, and exposure to a developing region of the financial gadget.

Industrial Real Estate Investment Trusts: Industrial REITs spend money on business properties which includes warehouses, distribution centers, manufacturing centers, and specific kinds of commercial buildings.

Just like healthcare REITS, business agency REITS also make cash with the resource of manner of leasing their homes to prolonged-time period tenants.

The REIT advantages from a steady circulate of condo profits, whilst the tenants enjoy the use of the houses for business corporation functions.

Industrial REITs can also moreover benefit from e-trade and logistics traits, because the boom of online shopping and the want for green distribution and garage centers, which commonly commonly tend to boom call for for commercial enterprise homes.

Lodging/Resorts Real Estate Investment Trusts: Lodging/Resorts Real Estate Investment Trusts (REITs) are a kind of REIT that invests in inns and inn homes.

These houses may additionally moreover encompass resorts, resorts, lodges, excursion rentals, and one of a kind styles of hospitality houses.

Lodging/Resorts REITs generally have excessive yields because the decision for for motels and lodge houses is specially strong as people excursion for business organisation and pride continuously.

Lodging/Resort REITs also can benefit from tourism dispositions and the increase of the travel organization.

However, because they'll be greater sensitive to economic and tourism traits, Lodging/Resort REITs may be extra volatile than incredible varieties of real property investments.

Self-storage Real Estate Investment Trusts: Self-storage Real Estate Investment Trusts (REITs) are a type of REIT that invests in self-storage facilities.

Individuals and groups can use those centers to hold assets which includes fixtures, documents, and different personal gadgets.

Customers benefit from a stable and on hand area to keep their belongings, at the same time as self-storage REITs earn earnings thru leasing the gadgets out to them.

Self-storage REITs are hundreds less volatile than specific forms of actual estate investments due to the reality call for for self-garage centers is distinctly strong, even throughout recessions.

In reality, inside the direction of financial downturns, name for for self-storage facilities might also moreover increase as individuals and corporations downsize or float to smaller regions.

Self-garage REITs can also advantage from demographic traits like urbanization and downsizing.

As extra people circulate into town regions and live in smaller areas, they'll need greater garage vicinity for his or her property.

In addition, as more infant boomers downsize their homes, they'll moreover want extra garage region for their belongings.

Retail Real Estate Investment Trusts: Retail Real Estate Investment Trusts (REITs) invest in retail houses inclusive of buying centers, department stores, and other varieties of retail houses. Tenants in retail houses might also consist of department stores, grocery shops, consuming places, and different retail corporations.

Retail REITs can provide excessive yields, but they are extra volatile than other types of actual belongings investments due to their sensitivity to economic inclinations and changes in purchaser behavior.

Chapter 2: Creating A Real Estate Investment Plan

Real property investment can be a useful challenge if finished efficaciously. However, developing a nicely-concept-out investment plan is critical in advance than diving into the market.

This monetary break will educate you the crucial thing steps to growing a a success actual belongings funding plan.

Setting Goals and Objectives

The first step to developing a viable actual property investment plan is to set your goals and targets.

Ask yourself what you want to gain out of your investment.

Your dreams can be brief-term or extended-time period, however make sure that they are unique and measurable.

Here are a few examples of real belongings funding goals:

To generate passive income from making an funding in REITs.

To buy and maintain shares of viable actual belongings investment trusts for extended-time period appreciation.

Once you have got set your dreams, you may set unique desires to help you reap them.

For instance, in case your reason is to generate passive profits from condo homes, your dreams can also encompass:

Purchasing a positive amount of stocks within a selected time body

Investing in shares that pay out dividends frequently to maximise coins waft

In addition to monetary goals, it is also critical to recollect non-economic goals, which incorporates the amount of time you are inclined to devote on your real estate investments, threat tolerance, and regular lifestyle desires.

Evaluating a Real Estate Investment Trust's Portfolio

Evaluating a REIT's portfolio will let you verify the high-quality of the homes in the portfolio.

This is essential to developing an informed investment choice, because the exceptional and overall performance of the REIT's houses may also have a huge impact on its monetary fitness and profitability

You can get a enjoy of methods attractive the homes are to capability tenants and the way well they'll be likely to perform over time through comparing elements which include vicinity, circumstance, and shape.

Here are some factors to appearance out for whilst comparing a actual belongings funding hold in thoughts's portfolio:

1.   Location Analysis

The region of the houses that the REIT owns is one of the maximum important elements to consider at the same time as evaluating a REIT portfolio.

You have to take into account the vicinity's demographics, modern and projected economic increase, and close by actual assets market developments.

Also, to get a higher experience of the functionality call for for apartment residences in the location, observe the records on things like population boom, pastime increase, and earnings tiers.

Demographics: When analyzing the demographics of the vicinity where the REITs houses are placed, a few key elements to don't forget encompass:

Population Growth: Ensure that maximum houses are positioned in regions with a growing population. Areas with developing populations usually tend to have a higher call for for actual belongings, leading to higher condominium expenses and assets values.

Age distribution: The age distribution of a place's populace can imply the call for for awesome varieties of real estate.

For example, a metropolis with a better percentage of older citizens may have a better populace of seniors who're downsizing or getting into senior dwelling centers, at the equal time as areas with a excessive share of younger households also can have a better call for for unmarried-circle of relatives homes.

Ensure that the sort of houses that the REIT invests in are homes that cater to the bulk of the populace of that area.

Suppose the REIT is constructing multi-level own family houses in an area with an getting older population. In that case, that could endorse that the REIT might probable have a problem earning income and making profits in that area.

Household Income: The median household earnings of an area can suggest the potential of citizens to pay lease or buy houses and also can impact the ability rental fees for unique sorts of homes.

Ensure that the median own family earnings of the residents of that vicinity is at the least near the national common or the not unusual for that country. This is a easy indicator that the citizens can manipulate to pay for their lease on the same time as due, and the REIT will haven't any hassle with income or coins float from their assets in that vicinity.

Employment Trends: Certify that the residences are centered in areas with sturdy employment boom and low unemployment fees.

Areas with sturdy employment boom have a propensity to have a higher name for for real property as humans float to the region for paintings and require housing.

Education Level: Also, make certain that the homes are in regions with a instead informed populace, as those lessons of human beings have a propensity to have higher incomes and may be much more likely to hire or buy higher-stop homes, this means that more capability profits for the REIT.

Generally, proper signs for an area's demographics can also furthermore include developing populations, diverse a long time and income degrees, robust employment boom, and a as an opportunity knowledgeable populace. In evaluation, horrible signs and symptoms can also encompass declining populations, a immoderate percentage of older residents, stagnant or declining employment, and occasional median own family incomes.

Current and Projected Income Growth: Economic increase can have an effect at the decision for for actual assets and the capability for lease will boom or belongings fee appreciation.

Some of the important thing factors to keep in mind encompass:

Gross Domestic Product (GDP): GDP measures the general price of products and services produced inner an area. Ensure that the REIT's homes are centered in regions with high GDP as they have a tendency to have strong financial increase, that might boom demand for real belongings.

Employment Trends: Look out for REITs with houses in areas with low unemployment charges and a developing assignment marketplace. These will be inclined to draw extra residents and organizations, which could growth call for for actual belongings.

Industry Diversification: Areas with a numerous combo of industries have a propensity to be extra resilient to economic downturns, as they are much less reliant on a unmarried zone.

Infrastructure Investments: Infrastructure investments, which includes new transportation or public centers, can lure new citizens and agencies, increasing demand for actual assets.

Projections: Economic projections, at the side of population increase or way boom, also can offer belief into the functionality name for for actual belongings in a place.

In precis, appropriate signs of an area's monetary boom might also additionally encompass excessive GDP increase, low unemployment charges, a various mixture of industries, and investments in infrastructure. In evaluation, lousy signs and symptoms often include declining GDP boom, excessive unemployment expenses, a lack of company range, and a lack of investment in infrastructure.

2.   Local Real Estate Market Trends

The nearby real belongings market developments can offer notion into the supply and demand of real property and assist determine if the vicinity is a top notch funding possibility.

When comparing a potential REIT to invest in, make sure that their houses are focused in areas with terrific trends within the neighborhood actual property marketplace.

Look out for elements like:

Vacancy Rates: High vacancy fees can propose an oversupply of real property within the location, leading to decrease apartment prices and assets values.

Rental Rates: Rental quotes can mean the extent of name for for actual assets inside the location. Rising condominium fees can endorse a growing call for for real belongings, even as declining rental expenses also can moreover recommend a shrinking name for.

Property Values: Property values can also provide notion into the overall health of the real assets marketplace. If assets values are developing in an area, it may suggest strong call for and restricted supply, on the same time as declining belongings values can propose oversupply or a lack of name for.

You need to make certain that the REITs homes aren't focused in areas with declining assets values.

Days on Market: The time body it takes for homes to promote or lease can provide notion into the decision for for real property within the place.

Again, bypass for REITs with most of their residences in excessive-name for areas.

New Construction: The quantity of latest production in the region can offer perception into the capability for oversupply inside the destiny.

As formerly stated, pretty a few advent in a place can suggest a immoderate call for for real property. Still, if there are too many new homes, name for also can overshoot deliver in the end, and developers may additionally moreover have a extra hard time taking benefit in their investments at the same time as such happens.

Generally, it might be terrific to choice REITs with most in their houses in areas with exceptional community real estate market inclinations which consist of low emptiness costs, growing rental charges, growing assets values, short days in the marketplace, and constrained new creation. Avoid REITs with extra of their houses in regions with immoderate vacancy prices, declining condo prices, declining property values, lengthy days in the marketplace, and a significant quantity of latest systems.

3.   Cashflow Analysis

Another essential detail to endure in thoughts is the cash waft generated with the resource of the homes within the REIT's portfolio.

You'll need to take a look at the rent roll for each belongings and examine the cash flow announcement to understand the internet working income (NOI) and the fee variety from operations (FFO).

This will provide you with an concept of the earnings generated by means of the REIT's homes and whether or not that earnings will likely expand or decline over time.

In the subsequent section, you may locate a sensible guide to try this clearly.

4.   Market Analysis:

In addition to looking at the neighborhood real assets market inclinations, you need to additionally hold in thoughts the broader market conditions.

This is composed of factors like hobby charges, inflation, and basic financial boom.

If interest costs are low, for instance, that could make borrowing less expensive for the REIT and help enhance its returns.

However, immoderate inflation need to erode the rate of the REIT's belongings and decrease its profitability.

5.   Financial Analysis

It's additionally essential to dig into the REIT's monetary statements to recognize its modern day monetary health.

You'll want to test matters just like the debt-to-equity ratio, the interest coverage ratio, and the price-to-profits ratio.

These metrics will give you a feel of the REIT's leverage, capacity to service its debt, and the way the marketplace values its earnings capability.

In the subsequent phase, you will discover a practical manual that will help you take a look at a REIT's monetary statements earlier than making an funding.

6.   Property   Standard   and   Structure Analysis

When evaluating the homes in the REIT's portfolio, it is vital to take into account their satisfactory and shape.

You'll want to have a have a study topics just like the age of the buildings, the scenario of the devices, and the extent of maintenance and safety required.

These elements can impact the portfolio's prolonged-term performance and capability for destiny expenses.

Age of the Buildings: Older houses can also require more maintenance and upkeep, which may be pricey. Additionally, older houses may additionally have previous centers and abilties, that would impact their ability to attract tenants.

Ensure that the houses in the REITs portfolio are not in maximum times aged and outdated houses.

Condition of the Units: The condition of the gadgets can also effect the selection for for the property and the functionality for lease will increase.

Units that require massive renovation or enhancements can be lots much less relevant to tenants and might require more funding to convey them up to traditional.

Level of Maintenance and Upkeep: The diploma of safety and protection required can impact the overall prices of the portfolio.

While houses with ultra-modern-day facilities and utilities can also look like in greater call for and provide more rewards, those houses might also moreover require ordinary safety, and upkeep may be more expensive to keep through the years, eroding the REITs' profits and, all the time, the ones of the consumers.

Capital Expenditures: Capital prices, which include changing roofs or HVAC structures, can be a huge charge for assets proprietors. It's essential to maintain in thoughts the potential for those sorts of prices at the identical time as comparing the capability returns of the portfolio.

Amenities and Features: The property's facilities and functions can impact its capability to draw and maintain tenants. Properties with current facilities, which incorporates fitness centers or outside areas, may be greater attractive to tenants and can command higher apartment fees.

Typically, suitable signs and symptoms and signs and symptoms while performing portfolio shape evaluation embody more current houses with modern-day-day centers, properly-maintained devices that require minimal maintenance, and a potential degree of preservation and renovation.

Conversely, horrible symptoms and symptoms may embody older houses that require vast renovation or upgrades, poorly maintained devices, and excessive protection and safety.

7.   Legal and Regulatory Analysis:

Finally, don't forget any criminal and regulatory troubles that would effect the REIT's operations.

This may additionally moreover need to consist of zoning prison hints, environmental rules, and tenant safety jail tips.

You'll want to ensure that the REIT complies with all applicable criminal guidelines and suggestions and has a plan in area to address any functionality jail or regulatory demanding conditions that may get up.

By thinking about the ones elements, you could determine whether or not or now not making an investment in a specific REIT is a superb in shape on your funding approach and chance tolerance.

Analyzing Financial Statements

This is a critical step in making an funding selection, whether or not in a REIT, ETF, or actual property mutual fund.

Here are a few key steps to test even as studying the economic statements of those varieties of investments:

1.   Review the Income Statement

This is a economic statement that gives facts approximately a agency's , fees, earnings and income over a high-quality period.

When analyzing the income assertion of a REIT, look for trends in earnings growth, running costs, and internet earnings.

Net Income

Net income is the difference most of the REIT's sales and fees, and it is a high-quality way to assess the profitability of the REIT.

The net income represents the quantity of profit the REIT has earned in any case expenses had been deducted.

To calculate the net earnings of a REIT, you subtract the total expenses from the general income.

Here's an instance of the way to calculate the net income the usage of a pattern earnings assertion:

Assume the subsequent income statement for a REIT:

2022

Rental Revenue $10,000,000

Management Fees $1,000,000

Other Income $500,000

Total Revenue $11,500,000

Operating Expenses $5,000,000

Depreciation and Amortization $2,000,000

Interest Expenses $one million

General   and   Administrative   Expenses
        $500,000

Total Expenses $8,500,000

Net Income $three,000,000

To calculate the internet income for this REIT, subtract the overall prices of $8,500,000 from the whole income of $11,500,000:

Net Income = Total Revenue - Total Expenses
Net Income = $11,500,000 - $eight,500,000
Net Income = $3,000,000

This   approach   that   the   REIT   earned $3,000,000 in profits for the period.

To use the internet earnings to make an funding preference, you should evaluate the internet profits to previous periods in addition to to important REITs within the equal corporation.

A higher net earnings than the preceding years or a internet profits higher than the business enterprise commonplace can also propose a more potent monetary ordinary overall performance. It may be a first rate sign for investors.

Revenue Growth

To decide income boom, you could use a vital calculation evaluating sales inside the modern-day period to the previous period.

The method for calculating earnings increase is:

Revenue Growth = (Current Period Revenue - Prior Period Revenue) / Prior Period Revenue

Here's an instance of the way to calculate revenue increase using a sample income statement:

Assume the subsequent income declaration for a REIT:

2022   2021

Rental Revenue $10,000,000 $9,000,000

Management Fees $a million $800,000

Other Income $500,000 $4 hundred,000

Total Revenue $11,500,000 $10,two hundred,000

To calculate the income growth for the REIT, you can use the method above:

Revenue Growth = ($eleven,500,000 - $10,2 hundred,000) / $10,two hundred,000

Revenue Growth = $1,300,000 / $10,two hundred,000

Revenue boom = 0.127 or 12.7%

This suggests that the REIT's sales grew by 12.7% from 2021 to 2022.

A high-quality earnings boom charge may be an tremendous sign, indicating that the REIT is producing extra income through the years.

But if, but, the income growth rate is horrible, it may be a signal of an in poor health employer.

Operating Expenses

Review the charges section of the earnings assertion and check the breakdown of charges thru manner of sophistication.

Pay hobby to prices like belongings manage and fashionable and administrative prices, as these can effect the REIT's profitability. You want to make certain that the REIT has a exceptional earnings-to-fee ratio.

The profits-to-fee ratio measures the proportion of a REIT's rental profits that is spent on strolling prices.

A decrease charge ratio suggests that the REIT is more green in managing its fees, that could bring about better internet running income (NOI) and in all likelihood higher returns for buyers.

A properly income-to-rate ratio for a REIT can range depending at the belongings type, location, and different factors; however, a ratio above 1 is typically considered higher.

A ratio above 1 suggests that the REITs income is better than its charges, on the same time as a ratio underneath 1 manner that costs are higher than income.

A ratio of 1 is not an incredible signal both, as meaning earnings and costs are same.

To calculate the income-to-charge ratio, you want to comply with those steps:

Determine Total Income: Add up all of the belongings of profits obtained over the length you're evaluating, in conjunction with a month or a one year.

Calculate Total Expenses: Add up all the fees you have got got incurred over the duration, collectively with running, administrative, and hobby costs.

Divide Total Income via way of Total Expenses: Divide the complete profits via the use of the complete expenses to get the earnings-to-cost ratio.

For instance, if the entire profits is $4,000,000 and the whole fees are $three,000 000, the earnings-to-charge ratio might be 1.33 (four,000,000 ÷ 3,000,000 = 1.33).

You should additionally be privy to the dividend payout ratio, it's the percentage of earnings paid to shareholders as dividends.

REITs have to distribute ninety% in their profits as dividends to shareholders so you want to make certain that this REIT complies with this rule.

Suppose a REIT has a internet earnings of $a hundred million and might pay its shareholders $ninety million in dividends. To calculate the dividend payout ratio, divide $90 million by the usage of $one hundred million:

Dividend Payout Ratio = Dividends Paid / Net Income

Dividend Payout Ratio = $90 million / $one hundred million

Dividend Payout Ratio = 0.Nine or ninety%

In this situation, the REIT's dividend payout ratio is ninety%, which means that it's miles dishing out ninety% of its net income to shareholders as dividends.

2.   Examine the Balance Sheet

The balance sheet offers records approximately a commercial enterprise agency's belongings, liabilities, and fairness at a selected factor in time.

Look for inclinations inside the price of the residences or securities held by using the investment and the extent of debt and equity financing.

Ensure that the rate of the REITs homes is developing and not dwindling. You ought to additionally confirm that they have an great to-fairness ratio = Total debt / Total. This ratio is an indicator of a REIT's economic leverage you arrive at it via the usage of dividing tremendous debt by using way of basic fairness.

Let's say a REIT has the subsequent balance sheet records:

Total debt: $500 million

Total fairness: $1,000 million

To calculate the debt-to-equity ratio, divide the REIT's fashionable debt through its famous fairness:

Total Debt divided through Total Equity

$500 million / $1,000 million

Debt-to-Equity Ratio = zero.Five

The REIT's debt-to-fairness ratio is zero.Five, because of this that it has $0.50 of debt for each $1 of fairness.

A decrease debt-to-equity ratio shows that the REIT is relying much less on debt financing and has a stronger economic role.

Also, examine the liquidity ratios, which embody the modern-day and quick ratios, to recognize the commercial enterprise organisation's short-term financial health.

The modern-day-day ratio is a degree of a REIT's liquidity and capacity to satisfy its brief-term money owed. It is calculated via dividing the REIT's property with the aid of the use of using its present day-day liabilities.

Suppose a REIT has the subsequent stability sheet facts:

Current Assets: $ hundred million

Current Liabilities: $100 million

To calculate the modern-day-day ratio, we might divide the REIT's modern-day property through its present day liabilities:

Current ratio = Current Assets / Current Liabilities

Current ratio = $two hundred million / $100 million

Current Ratio = 2

In this example, the REIT's present day ratio is 2, which means it has $2 of current property for each $1 of modern-day liabilities.

A cutting-edge ratio of or higher is typically taken into consideration correct, as it indicates that the REIT has ok short-time period property which could cater and meet its quick-term liabilities. The brief ratio is a extra conservative degree of a REIT's liquidity and potential to meet its brief-term money owed than the current ratio. It is calculated thru dividing the REIT's brief assets thru its cutting-edge liabilities.

Quick property encompass cash, marketable securities, and debts receivable.

Suppose a REIT has the subsequent stability sheet facts:

Quick Assets: $one hundred million

Current Liabilities: $50 million

To calculate the fast ratio, we would divide the REIT's short property by using its present day-day liabilities:

Quick ratio = Quick Assets / Current Liabilities

Quick ratio = $one hundred million / $50 million

Quick Ratio = 2

In this situation, the REIT's brief ratio is , that means it has $2 of brief property for every $1 of cutting-edge-day liabilities.

A short ratio of 1 or better is normally considered splendid, indicating that the REIT has sufficient liquid property to cover its short-term liabilities.

three. Analyze the Cash Flow Statement

The cash waft statement affords information about a agency's coins inflows and outflows over a particular length.

When reading a coins go with the flow declaration, it's essential to be aware about the assets and uses of cash within the working, making an investment, and financing sports sections.

The walking sports activities section represents the cash waft from the company's primary business enterprise operations, on the same time as the making an funding sports segment represents coins flows related to the acquisition and sale of lengthy-term property, which include assets and device.

The financing sports sports phase represents coins flows related to the enterprise's financing, which include the issuance or compensation of debt or equity.

Here's an instance of tactics to investigate the coins go with the waft declaration:

Suppose a REIT has the following cash flow announcement:

Cash Flows from Operating Activities: $50 million

Cash Flows from Investing Activities: -$20 million

Cash Flows from Financing Activities: -$10 million

To study this cash float assertion, you could first examine that the company generated $50 million from its strolling activities.

This shows that the business organization's number one commercial agency operations are producing remarkable cash flows, that is mostly a super signal.

Next, have a look at the making an investment sports section, which shows that the commercial enterprise agency spent $20 million on investments in lengthy-time period assets. This have to signify that the business agency is making an funding in future growth or upgrading its device and facilities.

Finally, have a examine the financing sports phase, which suggests that the enterprise repaid $10 million in debt or equity. This may want to endorse that the company is lowering its leverage or paying dividends to its shareholders.

Overall, this cash float statement indicates that the commercial agency organisation is producing powerful cash flows from its running sports activities and making an investment in its future increase at the equal time as moreover lowering its debt or fairness.

This will be a effective signal of the enterprise business enterprise's financial health and functionality for destiny boom.

four. Review Management's Discussion and Analysis (MD&A)

Management's Discussion and Analysis is a section of the economic statements that offers statement from management at the agency's monetary performance and destiny outlook.

When studying the MD&A of a REIT, look for insights into the agency's technique, and ensure that the agency's funding approach aligns together collectively with your personal funding technique and desires.

Also, pay attention to their evaluation of market situations and danger factors that might impact destiny standard performance.

5.   Comparison to Industry Benchmarks

Comparing the financial average overall performance of the funding to enterprise benchmarks can provide precious insights into its relative usual overall performance.

Look for statistics on the investment's ordinary performance compared to comparable investments, together with other REITs or actual property funding groups, and have a look at its popular performance relative to industry benchmarks together with the S&P 500 or the NAREIT Equity Index.

By reviewing the income declaration, balance sheet, coins go with the flow statement, portfolio of homes or securities, MD&A, and company benchmarks, you may advantage a better understanding of the investment's financial performance, boom functionality, and dangers.

It is critical to carry out some of those analyses often to make certain that your investment remains aligned with your investment goals and chance tolerance.

Key Metrics to Evaluate Real Estate Investment Trusts

When comparing Real Estate Investment Trusts (REITs), you want to do not forget several key metrics. These metrics let you inspect the financial fitness and increase functionality of a REIT and make knowledgeable funding picks.

Let's walk through some of the most essential metrics to evaluate REITs with sensible examples to illustrate their application.

1.   Funds from Operations (FFO)

FFO is a key metric used to degree the monetary preferred overall performance of REITs. It is calculated by together with another time depreciation and amortization expenses to net earnings and subtracting income from earnings of houses.

FFO provides a higher mirrored photo of a REIT's cash float than net income, because it considers that real assets property commonly respect over the years.

For example, shall we embrace you're thinking about making an investment in a retail REIT. The corporation stated a internet profits of $10 million for the 12 months but had $five million in depreciation and amortization prices and $2 million in profits from the sale of homes. Its FFO for the 365 days could be calculated as follows:

FFO = Net profits + Depreciation and amortization prices - Gains from earnings of houses

FFO = $10 million + $5 million - $2 million

FFO = $thirteen million

The REIT's FFO might be $13 million.

Next, calculate the organization's FFO ratio. The FFO (Funds From Operations) ratio is a diploma of a REIT's capability to generate coins from its center operations. It is calculated via manner of dividing the REIT's FFO with the resource of its widespread earnings.

Generally, a higher FFO ratio is taken into consideration better as it suggests that the REIT is generating greater coins from its operations.

As a tough guiding precept, a incredible FFO ratio for a REIT business enterprise is normally above 70%. However, this will variety considerably relying on the business enterprise and market conditions.

For example, REITs focusing on boom can also moreover have a lower FFO ratio as they reinvest more of their earnings into the industrial agency to fund their enlargement plans.

2. Price-to-FFO Ratio

The fee-to-FFO ratio is a valuation metric this is commonly used to assess the relative fee of severa REITs.

It is calculated through dividing the present day-day stock price with the resource of the agency's FFO in keeping with percentage.

For example, shall we embrace the retail REIT we mentioned in advance has a current-day stock fee of $50 consistent with percentage and an FFO in line with share of $3. Its charge-to-FFO ratio might be calculated as follows:

Price-to-FFO Ratio = Stock fee / FFO consistent with share

Price-to-FFO Ratio = $50 / $3

Price-to-FFO Ratio = 16.Sixty seven

This technique that the REIT's rate-to-FFO ratio is 16.Sixty seven, suggesting that the business agency's stock may be puffed up in evaluation to its FFO.

A fee-to-FFO ratio of above 20 is commonly considered appealing for REIT clients.

three. Dividend Yield

The dividend yield is a degree of the profits generated thru a REIT's dividends relative to its stock price.

Dividend Yield= The dividend regular with proportion (every year)/inventory price

For example, allow's expect the REIT can pay an annual dividend of $2 regular with percentage and has a modern-day inventory charge of $50 in keeping with percent. Its dividend yield is probably calculated as follows:

Dividend Yield = Annual dividend consistent with proportion / Stock rate

Dividend Yield = $2 / $50

Dividend Yield = 4%

The dividend yield may be four%, which shows that the enterprise employer can be a excellent income-producing investment.

A 2% to six% dividend yield is typically taken into consideration a super range for optimum customers. However, as we referred to, this will range widely relying on the agency, the economic agency agency's growth potentialities, and stylish marketplace conditions.

four.   Debt-to-Equity Ratio

The debt-to-equity ratio is a quantitation of a REIT's leverage or the amount of debt it has relative to its equity. It is calculated by means of dividing fashionable debt with the aid of manner of way of overall fairness.

Let's say the REIT has $one hundred million in primary debt and $ hundred million in widespread equity. Its debt-to-fairness ratio is probably calculated as follows:

Debt-to-Equity ratio = Total debt / Total equity

Debt-to-Equity ratio = $one hundred million / $ hundred million

Debt-to-Equity Ratio = 0.Five

The REIT's debt-to-equity ratio will be zero.Five, which may mean that the enterprise has a moderate quantity of debt relative to its fairness.

In contemporary, a debt-to-fairness ratio of 1 or tons less is taken into consideration properly, because it indicates that the agency has a lower level of debt relative to its equity.

A debt-to-fairness ratio of one approach that the company's common debt is equal to its wellknown equity. A lower ratio way that the agency has a lower diploma of debt, which commonly makes it an entire lot less volatile for traders.

However, it's miles critical to phrase that the proper debt-to-equity ratio can range depending on the business enterprise and agency version of the REIT.

5.   Occupancy Rates

Occupancy costs are a key metric for comparing REITs that very own and characteristic real property residences. This metric measures the share of available region currently leased or serious about the useful resource of way of tenants.

Chapter 3: How To Invest In Reits

Investing in REITs is a easy method as soon as you have executed your due diligence and are armed with a strong investment method.

Step One: Ensure That You Meet the Legal Requirements

The prison requirements for making an investment in a real assets investment consider may moreover range relying at the united states of america or jurisdiction you are in. However, in fashionable, investors are required to meet sure eligibility requirements to put money into mutual fee variety, which incorporates:

Accredited Investor Status: Some REITs can also best be available to accredited buyers, who want to fulfill positive profits or internet worth requirements set through securities regulators including the USA Securities and Exchange Commission (SEC).

To be taken into consideration an authorized investor, you need to either have:

A internet worth of as a minimum $1 million now not which encompass your number one house cost

An income of as a minimum $two hundred,000 in every of the 2 most present day years (or $three hundred,000 combined earnings with a spouse) and an expectation of undertaking the identical income degree in the present 3 hundred and sixty 5 days

Additionally, wonderful entities at the facet of businesses, partnerships, and trusts moreover may be considered authorized consumers inside the occasion that they have as a minimum $5 million in belongings or if all of their fairness owners are authorized investors.

Investor Documentation: Before investing in a REIT, you could want to complete documentation to verify your identity and funding eligibility. This might also include imparting your private records, collectively with a central authority-issued ID and Social safety information, and signing criminal agreements related to the funding.

Investment Restrictions: In a few states or global places, the amount of capital an man or woman or entity can put money into a REIT can be restrained. These regulations are designed to guard traders and make certain they do now not positioned too much in their capital at threat in a single investment.

It facilitates to decide if there are such restrictions to your united states or u.S.A. Of the united states so you can predetermine the amount of capital you are legally usual to place proper right into a REIT funding.

It may additionally additionally assist to discuss with a criminal or monetary expert in your community area so they permit you to understand the unique prison requirements for making an funding in a REIT for your locality.

Age Requirement: Investors should be of criminal age of their jurisdiction to enter into a settlement.

KYC (Know Your Customer) Compliance: Investment corporations are required to conform with Anti-Money Laundering (AML) and Counter-Terrorism Financing (CTF) legal guidelines and guidelines.

Therefore, you might be required to offer tremendous identification files and extraordinary relevant statistics to installation your identification.

Step Two: Determine Capital Requirements

The capital requirements for making an investment in a real assets investment keep in mind can range counting on the correct consider and the investment platform getting used.

For example, some REITs may additionally moreover require an initial funding of $1,000, on the same time as others can also additionally have a higher requirement of $25,000 or more.

It's critical to predetermine how a notable deal capital you have and are organized to install, as this will assist you even as you're searching for to pick out the proper buying and selling platform.

Suppose a platform has a minimum investment requirement of $5000, and also you simplest have $1,000 to make investments. In that case, you will probably have to select out a completely unique platform with a minimum funding requirement that suits your budget.

Step Three: Decide on the Type of REIT You Want to Invest In

As stated formerly, there are 3 one-of-a-type classes of REITs and the manner you'll maintain with making an investment relies upon at the type of REIT you need to spend money on.

Investing in Public REITs

This is just like purchasing a few different shares on the inventory change market.

If you do no longer have already got one, get an internet brokerage account. There are a couple of accurate ones, together with Charles Schwab, Fidelity Investments, TD Ameritrade, and eToro, to mention some.

Make certain you do large research in advance than registering with any on line brokerage, so that you don't fall into the fingers of scammers or brokerages that offer poor purchaser opinions.

You also are legally common to apply your employer-sponsored retirement account or specific tax-advantaged funding money owed, like man or woman retirement debts (IRAs), 401(ok)s, or health financial savings money owed (HSAs), to invest in public REITs.

Once you have a web brokerage account, studies REITs and take a look at them in advance than figuring out which of them to invest in.

Carefully undergo in thoughts elements similar to the returns and dividends they have got generated over the years, their portfolio and historic overall performance, the qualifications and experience of their control institution, the company's song report, and most significantly, liquidity.

You need to make certain that whatever REIT you're making an investment in may be effortlessly presented and provided on the stock exchange market so that you can without problem get proper of get entry to on your funding's cash fee at any time.

Investing in Public Non-Traded REITs

It's not as smooth to put money into unlisted public REITs as it's far to invest in publicly traded ones.

You may not be able to purchase the ones schooling of stocks thru your online brokerage account, so that you may also moreover have to shop for them immediately from the REIT organization or funding systems.

The drawback is that some systems have minimal investment necessities for public non-traded REITs, that would bypass as immoderate as $2,500.

You will also be required to keep on on your shares for as lots as 5 years or greater in advance than promoting them.

Again, the key's research. Make top notch you do large research in advance than making a decision to any platform or investment.

Investing in Private REITs

As noted previously, private REITs are surely certainly one of a type to legal traders or funding agencies, and their minimal purchase quantities can cross as excessive as $25,000.

If you need to invest in personal REITs, you should go through private provider-dealers.

But endure in mind that you will be carefully constrained at the kind of shares you can promote constant with time. This way, most times, you may only sell off a small part of your inventory with a large income price attached.

Their annual manipulate price expenses also have a propensity to be on the steep component.

All of those and the reality that there may be commonly constrained records to track preferred performance are why the ones types of investments are actually reserved for properly-heeled shoppers.

Step Five: Research and Choose a Platform

There are some of investment systems that offer get right of entry to to real property funding trusts.

Fundrise: Fundrise is a web platform that gives shoppers the possibility to spend money on actual property via masses of funding merchandise, which incorporates REITs.

The platform has a minimal funding of $500 and offers severa REITs focused on commercial corporation, residential, and blended-use houses.

The platform has obtained exceptional reviews for its client-tremendous interface, apparent charge shape, and funding performance.

RealtyMogul: RealtyMogul is every other online platform that offers clients get proper of access to to private market real assets investments, which incorporates REITs.

RealtyMogul has a minimal funding of $five,000 and gives quite quite a number REITs targeted on commercial enterprise and domestic properties.

Roofstock: Roofstock is each different on-line platform that lets in buyers to spend money on unmarried-family apartment houses through a REIT form.

The platform has a minimum investment requirement of $5,000 and gives REITs focused on residential houses positioned in the end of the usa.

Roofstock has moreover received extremely good evaluations for its customer-exceptional interface and robust funding ordinary performance.

Streitwise: Streitwise is a web platform that offers investors the opportunity to spend money on commercial enterprise real estate thru a publicly registered, non-traded REIT.

The platform specializes in office houses placed in excessive-growth markets at some stage in the us and has a minimal investment of $1,000.

Streitwise has received splendid reviews for its low charges and strong investment performance.

Rich Uncles: Rich Uncles is a web platform that offers customers the opportunity to invest in actual belongings via a publicly registered, non-traded REIT.

They interest on making an investment in diverse employer homes, together with workplace, retail, and business houses.

Rich Uncles has one of the lowest minimal funding portions of $500 and has acquired first-rate critiques for its obvious rate shape and robust investment average overall performance.

Step Six: Open an Investment Account

You can inspect any of these listed above but be sure to study the account necessities, charges, and minimum funding quantity for the platform in advance than you select out.

Step Seven: Choose a REIT

Once your funding account has been authorized on the platform, you can need to pick out a actual assets investment consider to put money into.

You can research one in every of a type ones on your chosen platform or use an internet fund screener to take a look at them.

Real assets investment trusts can range of their investment techniques, charges, and universal performance, so you'll want to investigate and observe unique options to determine which agencies align at the side of your dreams and hazard tolerance.

Step Eight: Fund Your Account

You will need to fund your account with capital to spend money on a REIT. The amount of capital required will rely upon your chosen platform and the REIT you want to invest in.

Funding your account is normally sincere. Most structures will in reality require you to connect your economic institution account or credit card on your account genuinely so you'll be capable of transfer charge variety backward and forward.

You may also be capable of fund your account via the usage of mailing a check to the brokerage organisation.

Step Nine: Purchase Shares

Once your account is funded, you should buy shares of the REIT you have got selected. This is generally completed thru the platform's trading interface, if you need to will will permit you to specify the range of shares you want to buy and the charge you're willing to pay.

Step Ten: Monitor your Investment

After making an funding in a REIT, it is essential to expose your investment to make certain it's miles performing as anticipated.

Keep an eye constant consistent on elements together with the REIT's dividend yield, internet asset price, and ordinary usual overall overall performance.

Step Eleven: Sell your Shares

If you decide to promote your shares in a REIT, you may do so through the equal platform you used to purchase them.

Depending at the platform and the best REIT, you may need to pay costs or commissions to sell your stocks.

Step Twelve: Pay Taxes

When you put money into a REIT, you ought to pay taxes on any dividends or capital profits you earn.

It lets in to visit a tax professional to understand your tax duties and a manner to document your funding earnings. Still, within the next chapter, we are going to deliver a cutting-edge-day manual to help you calculate and report taxes on profits earned out of your REIT funding.

Chapter 4: Building A Profitable Reit Portfolio

Throughout your investment adventure, it is critical to hold to show, readjust, and rebalance your portfolio to ensure that it stays profitable and maintains to align in conjunction with your funding dreams and goals.

Here are a few strategic techniques to make sure that your REIT portfolio stays worthwhile:

1.   Diversify your Portfolio

Diversification is key to decreasing danger on the identical time as making an funding in REITs. It lets in to put money into a combination of REITs that very very personal homes in extraordinary sectors and geographic places to limit the effect of any character REIT's wellknown overall performance to your regular returns.

2.   Rebalance your Portfolio Periodically

You need to moreover keep in mind rebalancing your portfolio every so often. This way eliminating non-performing property and replacing them with greater of the performing ones or making an funding cash in new belongings that display great functionality.

Periodically rebalancing your portfolio allows you keep your preferred risk-praise stability and make sure that your portfolio remains various and aligned together with your investment desires.

3.   Monitor your Investments Regularly

Keep a close to eye in your REIT investments, particularly tracking each REIT's financial fitness, growth opportunities, and everyday ordinary overall performance. This permits you to make knowledgeable choices on when to shop for, sell, or hold your investments.

4.   Stay up to date on Market Trends

Keep up to date on market trends and developments   inside   the   real   assets enterprise to make knowledgeable funding selections.

You can undergo in thoughts subscribing to company courses, attending meetings, and networking with distinct traders to stay knowledgeable.

5.   Consider each Public and Private REITs

While publicly traded REITs are the most commonplace, private REITs also can provide particular possibilities for diversification and probable better returns.

However, private REITs have more pointers and less liquidity than public REITs, so it is critical to carefully check those investments in advance than committing.

6.   Keep an Eye on Interest Rates

Interest prices can effect the general ordinary performance of REITs, as better prices can boom borrowing expenses for REITs and reduce name for for actual property.

Stay informed on hobby rate inclinations and adjust your portfolio as had to reduce the impact of growing charges.

7.   Take a Long-time period Approach

Investing in REITs is satisfactory performed with an extended-term method, as quick-time period volatility is fashionable within the market.

Avoid making impulsive selections based on brief-time period market actions and as an alternative cognizance at the lengthy-term boom ability of your investments.

8.   Consider the Overall Economy

The common health of the monetary gadget can effect the overall overall performance of REITs.

When making investment selections, maintain in mind macroeconomic factors consisting of unemployment fees, GDP increase, and inflation.

This allow you to become aware about potential opportunities and decrease chance for your portfolio.

nine.   Be Patient and Disciplined

Investing in REITs calls for patience and location. Don't get stuck up in brief-time period fluctuations within the marketplace, but as an opportunity, reputation on your prolonged-time period investment dreams and keep on together with your funding technique.

REIT Portfolio Diversification Strategies

Diversification refers to spreading your funding across multiple REITs that personal homes in remarkable sectors and geographic places.

This is completed to lessen the chance of your funding being centered in a unmarried belongings or vicinity. Diversification is vital because it can help you reduce the danger of dropping cash inside the occasion of a downturn in a single area or location.

Investing in a diverse portfolio of REITs can reduce the effect of any single REIT's common standard performance on your preferred funding returns.

Here are some diversification strategies you may use:

Diversify through the use of assets type: One manner to diversify your REIT portfolio is to put money into REITs that specialize in unique kinds of homes, which include office homes, buying facilities, or residences.

This will can help you spread your danger all through unique sectors and reduce the impact of any man or woman place's standard performance in your average portfolio.

Diversify with the resource of geographic vicinity: Investing in REITs that personal homes especially places is some exclusive way to diversify your portfolio.

This let you unfold your danger for the duration of awesome areas and reduce the impact of any area's economic performance for your portfolio.

Diversify with the resource of funding technique: REITs can lease specific investment strategies, along with fee making an funding or growth making an funding. Investing in REITs with various techniques of investment can diversify your portfolio and decrease the effect of someone funding technique's overall performance on your traditional portfolio.

Diversify via market capitalization: REITs may be categorised with the aid of marketplace capitalization, with huge-cap REITs having a marketplace capitalization of over $10 billion, mid-cap REITs having a marketplace capitalization among $2 billion and $10 billion, and small-cap REITs having a marketplace capitalization of below $2 billion.

By investing in REITs with one in every of a type marketplace capitalizations, you may diversify your portfolio and reduce the effect of any person market capitalization's performance on your commonplace portfolio.

Diversify by way of way of danger diploma: REITs also can style of their hazard tiers, with some REITs being extra conservative and others being extra competitive.

Consider making an funding in REITs with excellent threat ranges; you can diversify your portfolio and decrease the impact of any person threat diploma's normal performance to your ordinary portfolio.

Another way to diversify your REIT portfolio is to invest in ETFs or mutual price range protecting a remarkable REIT portfolio.

This will let you unfold your danger during a extra large type of investments and reduce the effect of any investment's common overall overall performance in your conventional portfolio.

By the use of the ones diversification strategies, you may assemble a worthwhile REIT investment portfolio that might withstand marketplace fluctuations and generate consistent returns over the long time.

Reinvesting Dividends for More Profits

Reinvesting dividends is a approach that allow you to maximize your income whilst making an funding in REITs. Here are a few methods you could reinvest your dividends for additonal profits:

1.   DRIPs: Many REITs offer dividend reinvestment plans (DRIPs), with a view to assist you to robotically reinvest your dividends to buy additional shares of the REIT. This can help you accumulate greater shares over time, increasing your capacity for lengthy-term income.

2.   Buy more shares: You also can reinvest your dividends by way of the usage of the usage of them to buy extra shares of the REIT manually so that you can take benefit of the compounding impact of reinvested dividends.

3.   Invest in other REITs: If you are looking to diversify your portfolio, you can reinvest

your dividends in distinctive REITs which you agree with have strong boom capability. This also can help you unfold your chance and possibly boom your returns over the years.

4.   Use dividends to pay down Debt: If you have got first-rate debt, which includes a mortgage or student loans, you could use your REIT dividends to pay down your debt. Doing this can be a way to lessen your hobby fees through the years and loose up extra money for making an investment in one-of-a-kind opportunities.

5.   Consider a dividend boom technique: Another approach for reinvesting your dividends is to focus on REITs with a records of steady dividend boom.

By reinvesting your dividends in the ones forms of REITs, you can probable maximize your prolonged-time period profits and build a sturdy, assorted portfolio through the years.

Future Outlook for REITs

The outlook for REIT making an funding seems terrific, especially for buyers who take a protracted-term, strategic technique.

As the area recovers from the COVID-19 pandemic, the real belongings marketplace is expected to rebound, especially in sectors which consist of workplace, retail, and hospitality, which were hit tough via manner of the pandemic. This need to benefit REITs that invest in the ones sectors.

Governments spherical the world are making an investment in infrastructure duties, which should create new possibilities for REITs that invest in infrastructure-related homes together with transportation hubs and logistics centers.

Chapter 5: Tax Considerations For Reit Investors

As an investor thinking about making an investment in a Real Estate Investment Trust (REIT), it's miles important to recognize the tax implications of this shape of investment.

The tax remedy of REITs may be complex, and there are remarkable tax issues that investors need to be aware of in advance than making an funding. REITs are generally now not trouble to federal profits tax on the corporation degree.

However, this does not imply that REIT consumers are virtually exempt from taxes. There are nevertheless several tax implications that buyers ought to be aware about.

Tax Treatment of Dividends

As an investor in a Real Estate Investment Trust (REIT), it is critical to recognize a manner to calculate and document taxes at the dividends earned from your funding.

REITs are required to distribute at the least ninety% of their taxable earnings to their shareholders. These distributions are normally taxable as regular income, problem to the investor's earnings tax price.

In assessment, licensed dividends from ordinary corporations are taxed at a decrease charge. However, there may be an exception for "licensed REIT dividends," which might be eligible for a lower tax rate if positive conditions are met.

To qualify, the REIT have to have held the assets for additonal than forty five days, and the investor need to have held the shares for added than ninety days.

Step 1: Determine the Total Amount of Dividends Received

The first step in calculating the taxes on REIT dividends is to determine the general quantity of dividends you received for the duration of the tax twelve months. This statistics should be suggested on Form 1099-DIV, which your brokerage business enterprise usually gives.

In this situation, permit's expect you obtained $1,000 in dividends from a REIT in some unspecified time in the destiny of the tax 12 months.

Step 2: Determine the Type of Dividends Received

The subsequent step is to decide the kind of dividends you acquired. REIT dividends can be labeled as both "certified" or "non-licensed."

Qualified dividends are state of affairs to a decrease tax fee, whilst non-qualified dividends are charged on the everyday profits tax charge.

To be taken into consideration a qualified dividend, the REIT need to have met excessive first-class shielding duration requirements, and also you ought to have held the shares for a high-quality time frame. If the REIT meets those necessities, the dividends can be stated as qualified on Form 1099-DIV.

For instance, allow's count on that $800 of the $1,000 in dividends you received from the REIT were labeled as certified dividends.

Step 3: Determine the Tax Rate for Each Type of Dividend

Once you've got were given were given determined the shape of dividends you acquired, you need to decide the tax fee for each kind. For certified dividends, the tax price will rely upon your income degree and filing popularity. For the tax year 2022, the tax fees for certified dividends are as follows:

zero% tax rate for humans with taxable income as loads as $40,400 ($eighty,800 for married couples submitting collectively)

15% tax charge for humans with taxable income among $forty,401 and $445,850 ($eighty,801 and $501,six hundred for married couples filing together)

20% tax fee for humans with taxable profits above $445,850 ($501,601 for married couples submitting collectively)

For non-licensed dividends, the tax fee is primarily based absolutely in your normal profits tax rate.

For example, shall we embrace you're a unmarried filer with a taxable income of $50,000. Your tax price for certified dividends is probably 15%, at the same time as your tax price for non-certified dividends is probably your everyday income tax rate (it truly is 22% for taxable earnings among $forty,126 and $eighty 5,525).

Step four: Calculate the Taxes Due for Each Type of Dividend

Once you've got were given had been given determined the tax fee for each dividend kind, you may calculate every tax due. To calculate the taxes due for qualified dividends, multiply the certified dividends by way of the tax price.

For example, the use of the numbers from the preceding steps, you'll owe $one hundred twenty in taxes on the $800 of certified dividends you received ($800 x 0.15).

To calculate the taxes due for non-licensed dividends, you will want to multiply the amount of non-licensed dividends by means of your normal earnings tax rate.

For example, if your regular profits tax charge is 22%, you will owe $forty 4 in taxes at the $200 non-licensed dividends you acquired ($two hundred x zero.22).

Step 5: Report Dividend Income on Your Tax Return

Finally, you want to record your dividend income in your tax go once more. The general quantity of dividends acquired need to be stated on Form 104 0, while the quantity of qualified dividends and non-certified dividends need to be cautioned one after the alternative on Form 1099-DIV.

On Form 1040, dividend earnings is usually recommended on Line 3b. You need to moreover be a part of Schedule B in your tax go back if you obtained more than $1,500 in taxable hobby or ordinary dividends or had sure foreign bills or trusts.

Using the example from earlier, you may report $1,000 in dividend income on Line 3b of Form 1040 and fix Form 1099-DIV in your tax skip once more. You might probably furthermore want to separately file the $800 of licensed dividends and $2 hundred of non-certified dividends on Form 1099-DIV.

Tax Treatment of Capital Gains

Capital earnings tax is a tax on the profits you earn from promoting a capital asset, including shares or real property.

In the context of REIT making an funding, capital income tax can exercise while you promote your shares of a REIT for a income.

When you sell your shares of a REIT for a income, you'll owe capital profits tax at the distinction a number of the sale and buy costs.

This is what's known as 'capital profits.'

The amount of capital profits tax you owe is based upon on numerous elements, together at the side of your tax bracket, how prolonged you held the funding, and whether or now not the benefit is assessed as quick-term or lengthy-time period.

If you held your REIT investment for more than one three hundred and sixty five days in advance than promoting, the gain is taken into consideration lengthy-term and taxed on the tax price for long-term capital income. Long-time period capital earnings tax price is usually lower than the fast-term capital profits tax rate, which applies to investments held for twelve months or masses less.

It is essential to have a observe that REITs can also distribute capital profits to shareholders, which might be taxed on the equal rate due to the truth the investor's everyday profits tax rate. These capital income distributions are said on Form 1099-DIV and ought to be included on your annual tax cross lower back.

If you promote your REIT shares at a loss, you may be able to use the capital loss to offset other capital gains, lowering your common tax prison duty. Any more capital losses may be used to counterbalance up to $3,000 of annual regular income, with the residual losses carried onward to the destiny tax years.

Calculating Capital Gains Tax

To calculate capital income tax to your REIT investment, you could need to decide your price basis and the promoting fee.

Your cost foundation is the specific rate you paid for the shares plus any costs or commissions paid to shop for them.

For instance, permit's count on you obtain one hundred stocks of a REIT for $20 consistent with percentage and paid $10 in charges and commissions. Your general rate basis could be $2,010 (one hundred shares x $20 in step with percent + $10 in expenses).

If you later supplied those one hundred stocks for $30 in line with percentage, your selling rate may be $three,000.

Your capital benefit may be the difference amongst your promoting price and your charge foundation, which in this situation is $990 ($3,000 - $2,010).

Reporting Capital Gains Tax

To file capital income tax for your REIT investment, you may need to use Schedule D of Form 1040. On Schedule D, you'll listing all your capital earnings and losses for the twelve months, along with the ones from promoting your REIT stocks.

In the example above, you'll record the $990 capital gain on Schedule D and each different capital gains or losses you incurred in the path of the yr.

If you held the REIT shares for a couple of 12 months earlier than selling, the advantage may be taken into consideration a long-time period capital advantage and taxed at the prolonged-term capital gains tax charge. If you held the shares for 12 months or much less, the advantage may be taken into consideration a brief-term capital advantage and taxed at your everyday income tax charge.

For the 2022 tax one year, the tax expenses for the long-time period capital income are as follows:

0% for taxpayers within the 10% or 12% tax brackets

15% for taxpayers inside the 22%, 24%, 32%, or 35% tax brackets

20% for taxpayers inside the 37% tax bracket

If your ordinary taxable income is below the 15% tax bracket threshold, you may not owe any capital earnings tax for your lengthy-time period earnings. If your regular taxable profits is above the 20% tax bracket threshold, you can owe the maximum 20% long-time period capital earnings tax price for your profits.

If you have got every capital profits and capital losses for the yr, you can use your losses to offset your earnings, reducing your average tax prison obligation. Any extra capital losses may be carried in advance to destiny tax years.

It's vital to note that in case you sell your REIT shares for a loss, you may use the capital loss to counterbalance every other capital income for the three hundred and sixty five days or as much as $3,000 of regular earnings. Any residual capital losses can be carried ahead to destiny tax years.

Treatment of Depreciation

Real estate houses are usually challenge to depreciation for tax capabilities, which lets in clients to deduct a part of the assets's rate every 12 months.

Depreciation is an accounting technique utilized by REITs to spread the charge of a belongings over its beneficial existence for tax functions. Essentially, it lets in the REIT to deduct a part of the property's charge from its taxable income each yr.

In the context of REIT investment, depreciation need to have a huge impact on an investor's tax legal responsibility.

When a REIT opinions its taxable earnings, it must account for the depreciation deduction, which reduces its taxable earnings and, in flip, the quantity of tax it owes.

As a forestall end result, depreciation can help to lower a REIT's tax invoice, which can also moreover moreover cause higher dividends for customers. To offer a realistic instance, let's anticipate a REIT purchases a assets for $10 million, with an anticipated beneficial lifestyles of 30 years.

The REIT can use the depreciation method to spread the fee of the belongings over those 30 years.

Assuming a proper away-line depreciation method, the REIT should deduct $333,333 from its taxable profits every three hundred and sixty five days ($10 million divided through 30 years).

In this situation, the REIT's taxable income will be reduced through $333,333 each year, that may result in a decrease tax prison obligation. This, in flip, should allow the REIT to pay higher dividends to investors.

It's important to word that at the same time as depreciation can surely impact a REIT's tax criminal obligation and dividend bills, it is able to moreover complicate tax reporting for investors. When a REIT reviews its taxable earnings, it includes the depreciation deduction, making it hard for investors to decide their tax felony responsibility on REIT dividends and capital profits.

To calculate the quantity of depreciation that applies to your REIT funding, you could have a look at the REIT's financial statements, in particular the depreciation and amortization charges section. This will display the quantity of depreciation that the REIT has taken on its homes at some stage in the yr.

As an investor, you can deduct your share of the REIT's depreciation fee out of your taxes. To determine your percent, you need to understand the share of the REIT that you own. This facts can be found on your investment statements or via contacting your provider or economic advertising consultant.

For instance, permit's anticipate you private 1,000 shares of a REIT, and the REIT's depreciation price for the twelve months turn out to be $1 million. The REIT has a total of 10,000 stocks extremely good, which means you very very personal 10% of the REIT (1,000 stocks ÷ 10,000 standard shares). Therefore, your proportion of the depreciation charge is probably $one hundred,000 (10% x $1 million).

You can then deduct this quantity from your taxable earnings whilst reporting taxes in your REIT investment.

It's critical to study that depreciation is taken into consideration a passive pastime, this means that it may be trouble to passive loss boundaries. This way that you can not be able to deduct the whole quantity of the depreciation charge in a given 12 months, counting on your regular passive profits and losses.

It's commonly a splendid idea to are looking for advice from a tax professional or financial advertising consultant whilst reporting taxes for your REIT funding, especially almost about depreciation and specific complex tax troubles. They assist you to navigate the tips and make certain which you maximize your tax blessings at the same time as complying with tax laws.

How to Avoid Double Taxation

Double taxation inside the context of REIT making an investment refers back to the capacity for REIT dividends to be taxed instances: as soon as at the organisation diploma and another time at the person investor level.

Because REITs are set up as pass-thru entities, they do not pay corporation profits tax at the earnings they distribute as dividends. Instead, the tax legal responsibility is handed without delay to the man or woman clients who gather the dividends.

Thus, a few traders may moreover face double taxation within the event that they preserve their REIT shares in a taxable account.

This is due to the fact the dividends received from the REIT are taxed at the character degree as regular income, similar to another dividend.

In addition, the REIT also can be hassle to a tax called the covered profits tax (BIG tax) if it sells nice belongings within a certain time body. The BIG tax is a company-degree tax that might similarly reduce the amount of income to be had for distribution to shareholders as dividends.

To mitigate the ability for double taxation, do not forget making an investment in a tax-advantaged account like an IRA or 401(accurate sufficient). These debts will let you defer taxes to your funding earnings until you withdraw the price range in retirement. This will permit you to keep away from paying taxes in your REIT dividends on the individual diploma.

Another choice is to invest in REITs based totally as partnerships, which are not problem to corporate earnings tax and therefore do now not face the same double taxation problems.

Tax Planning Strategies for REIT Investors

As a REIT investor, you may use severa tax planning techniques to decrease your tax felony duty and maximize your after-tax returns.

Here are a few techniques to bear in mind:

Utilize Tax-loss Harvesting: If you have got were given investments that have misplaced rate, you can promote them and use the losses to offset any income you have made in other investments.

This is known as tax-loss harvesting, and it allow you to reduce your ordinary tax jail duty.

For example, when you have a $5,000 loss on one investment and a $five,000 advantage on every other, you could sell every and offset the gains with the losses, ensuing in no tax prison responsibility at the income.

Use a Tax-Deferred Exchange: If you want to promote a REIT funding and reinvest the proceeds in a few different REIT, you may use a tax-deferred change, moreover called a 1031 alternate.

This allows you to defer paying taxes on any profits you have were given made at the investment till you sell the contemporary-day funding.

For example, if you promote a REIT investment for $one hundred,000 and reinvest the proceeds in every other REIT, you could defer paying taxes on any gains until you promote the brand new investment.

Consider making an investment in a Roth IRA: Another option is to put money into a Roth IRA, which permits your cash to increase tax-loose and gives tax-loose withdrawals in retirement.

While you won't get a direct tax deduction for contributions to a Roth IRA, you will keep away from paying taxes on the investment profits inside the future.

For example, if you invest $10,000 in a Roth IRA and it grows to $20,000, you might not need to pay taxes at the $10,000 in earnings whilst you withdraw it in retirement.

Chapter 6: Definition Of Reits

Real Estate Investment Trusts, or REITs, are groups that personal or finance income-generating actual property houses. They have been created with the aid of the usage of manner of Congress in 1960 as a way for character customers to put money into huge-scale, income-generating real belongings, which includes condo homes, place of job homes, retail homes, and enterprise centers, even as now not having to buy, manage, or finance the houses themselves.

REITs are required with the resource of regulation to distribute at least ninety% in their taxable earnings to shareholders as dividends, making them an attractive funding for earnings-searching for shoppers. As a result, REITs can provide specifically immoderate dividend yields in evaluation to extraordinary stocks, and may offer a normal movement of profits to consumers.

To qualify as a REIT, a employer have to meet positive requirements set forth via the

Internal Revenue Service (IRS). For example, at the least 75% of a REIT's property ought to be invested in actual property, and at least seventy five% of the REIT's gross earnings have to come from actual belongings rents, interest on mortgages financing real belongings, or gains from the sale of actual estate belongings.

There are also unique kinds of REITs, which incorporates equity REITs, which very very own and function income-generating actual assets, and loan REITs, which invest in actual property debt, which includes mortgages and mortgage-backed securities. Some REITs can also consciousness on precise varieties of houses, which consist of inns, self-garage centers, or healthcare centers, even as others may also additionally invest in a big kind of belongings kinds.

Overall, REITs can offer person consumers a manner to spend money on earnings-generating actual estate, with the functionality for regular income and extended-time period capital appreciation. However, as with every funding, there are dangers involved, together with marketplace and monetary situations, interest charge fluctuations, and functionality modifications in tax felony recommendations and recommendations.

Brief records of REITs

Real Estate Investment Trusts, or REITs, had been created through Congress in 1960 as a part of the Cigar Excise Tax Extension, which was enacted to help spur economic boom and sell investment in the U.S. Economic tool. The motive of the REIT policies turn out to be to provide a manner for man or woman buyers to invest in big-scale, profits-generating actual assets, even as additionally providing a brand new supply of capital for the real assets employer.

At the time, there have been concerns that smaller customers were being excluded from making an investment in huge, income-generating real assets responsibilities due to the excessive price of get entry to and manipulate. The REIT form became designed to permit man or woman traders to pool their cash together to put money into actual assets, at the same time as furthermore imparting diversification and professional control.

In the early days of REITs, the organisation come to be particularly small and in huge component unknown to maximum buyers. However, over the years, the REIT shape have end up more well-known, and the employer started to increase. In 1992, the National Association of Real Estate Investment Trusts (NAREIT) have become mounted to assist promote the REIT industry and constitute the hobbies of REITs and their shareholders.

Over the years, the REIT organisation has continued to conform and increase, with new forms of REITs rising and the enterprise agency becoming more and more mainstream. Today, REITs are an essential a part of the real property and investment landscape, with billions of bucks in assets under control and tens of tens of millions of character customers taking part in the agency.

Overall, the facts of REITs is truely considered one of innovation and growth, because the commercial enterprise corporation has endured to comply and evolve to satisfy the desires of investors and the actual belongings marketplace.

Overview of methods REITs artwork

Real Estate Investment Trusts, or REITs, artwork by the usage of using allowing individual investors to pool their cash collectively to put money into profits-generating real property, on the equal time as additionally presenting professional manage and diversification.

When an man or woman invests in a REIT, they are essentially searching for stocks in a enterprise organisation that owns and operates profits-producing real property houses. The REIT then uses the price range raised from consumers to shop for and manage actual estate assets, in conjunction with rental buildings, workplace homes, searching for centers, and business residences.

As a shareholder in a REIT, buyers revel in the rental income generated by the underlying homes, further to any earnings determined out from the sale of these houses. REITs are required with the useful resource of regulation to distribute at least ninety% of their taxable income to shareholders inside the form of dividends, which could provide a steady flow of earnings to investors.

One of the crucial thing benefits of creating an funding in REITs is they offer diversification, as buyers can gain publicity to a splendid type of actual property assets and property types with a pretty small investment. Additionally, due to the fact REITs are traded on essential stock exchanges, they'll be as an opportunity liquid, which means that that that clients can purchase and promote shares consequences and quick.

Another advantage of REITs is they provide get right of entry to to big-scale, earnings-generating actual property assets that is probably tough or impossible for person investors to gather on their very own. REITs moreover offer expert control and facts, which can assist to reduce the risks related to investing in actual property.

Overall, REITs offer individual buyers a way to invest in earnings-producing actual belongings with fantastically low costs and risks, on the same time as moreover providing diversification, professional control, and liquidity. However, like every investment, there are risks involved, together with market and financial situations, hobby rate fluctuations, and potential adjustments in tax crook recommendations and guidelines. It is vital for clients to do their studies and are searching for advice from a economic marketing consultant earlier than making an funding in REITs.

Chapter 7: Diversification Benefits

One of the vital component advantages of investing in Real Estate Investment Trusts (REITs) is the diversification benefits they will be able to provide. Diversification is the exercising of spreading investments throughout pretty some property to lessen the risk of a person funding negatively impacting a portfolio.

REITs can provide diversification blessings in a number of strategies. First, REITs permit investors to advantage exposure to a considerable range of real property property and property kinds with a enormously small investment. This can help to lessen the threat of over-interest in a single property or real estate market, which may be a task for individual investors who are making an funding without delay in actual estate.

Second, because REITs are publicly traded, they offer traders the functionality to resultseasily buy and sell shares, providing liquidity and flexibility. This can assist to lessen risk in a portfolio thru the usage of allowing shoppers to rapid and without troubles alter their investments as marketplace conditions trade.

Third, because of the truth REITs can very very very own and characteristic actual estate houses in extraordinary geographic places and marketplace sectors, they are able to assist to reduce exposure to specific nearby or region-particular dangers. For example, if one region or sector studies a downturn, the various nature of a REIT portfolio can help to mitigate the impact of those risks.

Fourth, because of the reality REITs can invest in numerous property sorts, inclusive of residential, business, retail, and enterprise, they are able to provide publicity to one in all a type asset instructions and markets. This can help to lessen commonplace risk in a portfolio with the aid of using providing exposure to more than one sectors and markets.

Overall, the diversification blessings of REITs can assist to reduce risk in a portfolio via offering publicity to an entire lot of actual assets property, markets, and sectors. However, it is important to have a look at that no funding is without danger, and investors want to constantly do their studies and speak with a financial advertising representative earlier than investing in REITs or a few one of a kind funding.

Potential for immoderate dividends

Real Estate Investment Trusts (REITs) are required via using regulation to distribute as a minimum ninety% in their taxable profits to shareholders in the form of dividends, that could provide a normal circulate of profits to shoppers. As a give up end result, REITs can provide pretty excessive dividend yields in assessment to different stocks and investment options, making them an attractive preference for income-looking for buyers.

The excessive dividend yields of REITs can be attributed to a range of of factors. First, the earnings generated with the beneficial resource of the underlying actual belongings property can be good sized, especially in the case of houses with lengthy-term rentals or excessive occupancy costs. This income is then allotted to shareholders within the shape of dividends, imparting buyers with a regular go with the flow of income.

Second, due to the reality REITs are required to distribute at the least 90% of their taxable profits to shareholders, they have got a higher payout ratio than most unique shares. This can help to make REITs an attractive funding for buyers who are searching out a dependable supply of profits.

Third, the form of REITs can also contribute to their immoderate dividend yields. Because REITs are required to distribute their taxable profits to shareholders, they do no longer must pay organisation earnings taxes. This can assist to lessen the tax burden on the profits generated by using the usage of the underlying real property assets, thinking of better dividend payouts to shareholders.

Overall, the capability for immoderate dividends is a key attraction of creating an funding in REITs. However, it is vital to note that the immoderate yields of REITs come with certain dangers, together with marketplace and monetary conditions, hobby price fluctuations, and capability modifications in tax laws and tips. As with any investment, traders must do their studies and are looking for recommendation from a monetary representative in advance than making an funding in REITs or every special funding alternative.

Access to real estate without proudly proudly owning assets

One of the essential difficulty advantages of making an funding in Real Estate Investment Trusts (REITs) is that they provide get admission to to actual assets investments without requiring traders to non-public or manage physical property. This can be in particular attractive to consumers who're interested in the capacity benefits of actual belongings making an investment, but who do not want the duties or expenses related to proudly owning and handling bodily houses.

By making an investment in REITs, people can advantage publicity to the income-generating capability of real property property, such as homes which incorporates condominium houses, place of business buildings, retail regions, and industrial facilities. REITs are primarily based to allow character consumers to pool their fee variety collectively to put money into the ones belongings, which can be then managed with the useful resource of the REIT's control group.

Because REITs are professionally controlled, consumers do not must fear about the normal obligations of proudly owning and dealing with bodily houses. Instead, the control company of the REIT is responsible for handling the houses, accumulating rents, and managing renovation and maintenance. This can be a large gain for consumers who are seeking out a arms-off method to actual belongings making an investment.

Investing in REITs also can offer get entry to to a far broader type of real property investments than might be feasible for man or woman investors on their non-public. REITs can put money into a number of belongings types and markets, offering buyers with publicity to wonderful asset education and marketplace sectors. Additionally, due to the reality REITs are publicly traded, they may be fantastically liquid, because of this that customers can outcomes buy and promote stocks within the REIT as wished.

Overall, the functionality to get admission to actual assets investments without proudly proudly owning physical belongings is a significant gain of making an funding in REITs. By pooling price range together with exceptional consumers, people can advantage exposure to the earnings-producing capability of real estate property, on the same time as profiting from expert manipulate, diversification, and liquidity.

Potential for capital appreciation

In addition to providing earnings in the shape of dividends, Real Estate Investment Trusts (REITs) additionally offer the ability for capital appreciation. Capital appreciation refers to an increase in the price of an asset over the years, that may bring about a profits while the asset is sold.

The functionality for capital appreciation in REITs is tied to the fee of the underlying real property assets owned with the aid of manner of the REIT. If the fee of these belongings will increase through the years, the rate of the REIT's shares may additionally additionally furthermore boom, resulting in capital appreciation for consumers.

There are lots of of factors that might make contributions to capital appreciation in REITs. For instance, if the actual property market is strong and phone for for real assets is immoderate, the cost of the underlying homes owned with the aid of the REIT may moreover increase, predominant to a upward thrust within the rate of the REIT's stocks.

Additionally, if the REIT is ready to build up new homes or develop modern-day houses, this will moreover make contributions to capital appreciation. By inclusive of new property to the portfolio, the REIT can likely boom the general price of its holdings and generate greater profits.

It's crucial to word that, like all funding, there are risks associated with investing in REITs that would negatively effect capital appreciation. For example, monetary downturns or shifts inside the actual property market need to purpose a decrease in the fee of the underlying homes owned with the useful aid of the REIT, resulting in a decline in the charge of the REIT's stocks.

Overall, the potential for capital appreciation is each special capability gain of making an funding in REITs. While profits within the shape of dividends is the primary deliver of pass returned for plenty REIT customers, the capacity for capital appreciation can offer extra returns and benefits over the lengthy-time period.

Chapter 8: Equity Reits

Equity Real Estate Investment Trusts (REITs) are a sort of REIT that invests in and operates profits-generating actual property homes. Equity REITs personal and control homes along side workplace houses, buying facilities, condo houses, and commercial centers, with the purpose of manufacturing income from apartment income and capital appreciation.

As proprietors of profits-generating actual estate houses, equity REITs derive earnings from hire paid thru tenants. Equity REITs might also moreover private and manage a unmarried belongings or a portfolio of homes, and they will popularity on precise forms of houses or belongings sectors, which consist of healthcare or commercial actual assets. Equity REITs may also moreover spend money on homes located particularly geographic regions or markets.

Equity REITs generally generate profits for traders within the shape of dividends. The income generated with the aid of the use of the underlying actual property houses is sent to shareholders as dividends, which can be regularly higher than the dividends paid with the useful aid of different types of shares. This ought to make equity REITs an attractive funding for income-looking for traders who are seeking out a supply of ordinary, dependable earnings.

Equity REITs furthermore offer the ability for capital appreciation. If the value of the underlying real property houses will increase over the years, the rate of the equity REIT's stocks may moreover boom, ensuing in capital appreciation for buyers.

It's essential to examine that, like every investment, there are dangers related to making an investment in equity REITs. Market and financial situations, shifts in the real property marketplace, and adjustments in hobby fees or tax legal guidelines can all impact the performance of equity REITs. Additionally, equity REITs can be scenario to risks associated with property management, collectively with tenant turnover, protection and repair prices, and property damage or destruction.

Overall, equity REITs are a famous way for consumers to advantage publicity to income-generating real belongings houses at the same time as no longer having to non-public and manage bodily assets. By making an investment in equity REITs, buyers can doubtlessly benefit from steady income, capital appreciation, and professional manipulate of real property assets.

Mortgage REITs

Mortgage Real Estate Investment Trusts (REITs) are a form of REIT that invests in and manages real belongings debt, together with mortgages and loan-backed securities, in preference to bodily actual property homes. Mortgage REITs make cash with the aid of incomes hobby at the loans they make or the securities they preserve.

Unlike fairness REITs, which generate income from rental earnings and capital appreciation, loan REITs derive profits from interest earned on mortgage loans and mortgage-backed securities. Mortgage REITs might also additionally spend money on splendid forms of mortgage debt, which encompass residential and business mortgages, in addition to government-backed loan securities which encompass Fannie Mae and Freddie Mac.

Mortgage REITs generally generate profits for investors inside the shape of dividends, just like equity REITs. However, due to the fact the earnings generated thru mortgage REITs is tied to hobby prices, the dividend payouts from mortgage REITs can be more variable than the ones from equity REITs. In addition, due to the truth the mortgage marketplace may be greater volatile than the real belongings market, mortgage REITs can be undertaking to better levels of threat.

Mortgage REITs can also offer some benefits to shoppers. For example, loan REITs can doubtlessly benefit from the spread most of the hobby expenses on their mortgage investments and their private borrowing fees. Additionally, loan REITs can be masses tons less touchy to changes in real property market conditions, thinking about the fact that they may be now not depending on condominium profits or belongings values.

It's vital to phrase that, like severa investment, there are dangers associated with making an investment in loan REITs. Market and economic conditions, interest rate fluctuations, and modifications in regulatory and tax prison hints can all impact the general overall performance of loan REITs. Additionally, loan REITs may be trouble to credit rating hazard, this is the threat that the borrowers on their mortgage loans will default.

Overall, loan REITs are a specialized form of REIT that might offer earnings-searching for customers publicity to real property debt as opposed to bodily homes. By making an funding in mortgage REITs, buyers can likely benefit from earnings within the shape of dividends, as well as some diversification blessings and ability capital appreciation. However, traders need to cautiously do not forget the dangers associated with mortgage REITs in advance than making an investment on this kind of REIT.

Hybrid REITs

Hybrid Real Estate Investment Trusts (REITs) are a form of REIT that mixes factors of every fairness REITs and loan REITs. Hybrid REITs put money into each physical real assets residences and real belongings debt, which consist of mortgages and mortgage-backed securities.

Because hybrid REITs invest in each real property assets and real estate debt, they may be capable of provide a mixture of both earnings and capital appreciation capability. The income generated through the underlying homes and the hobby earned on the actual property debt can each make contributions to the general returns of the hybrid REIT.

Hybrid REITs can spend money on a number of assets sorts and real assets debt devices, together with business and home houses, authorities-backed loan securities, and privately issued mortgage debt. By making an investment in a aggregate of actual property assets and debt, hybrid REITs can probable offer traders diversification blessings and reduced volatility in evaluation to natural equity or loan REITs.

Like special styles of REITs, hybrid REITs generate income for buyers inside the shape of dividends. However, the dividend payouts from hybrid REITs can be more variable than the ones from natural equity REITs, for the reason that earnings generated with the aid of hybrid REITs is tied to each condo profits and hobby prices. Additionally, because of the truth hybrid REITs invest in each real assets belongings and debt, they'll be problem to both real assets market and credit score risks.

Overall, hybrid REITs can offer consumers exposure to every actual assets assets and debt, potentially imparting a aggregate of profits and capital appreciation functionality. However, consumers must cautiously maintain in thoughts the risks associated with hybrid REITs in advance than making an funding, as they may be problem to extra volatility and chance than herbal equity or mortgage REITs.

Chapter 9: Non-Public Reits

Private REITs, then again, are commonly wonderful available to widely wide-spread shoppers. Accredited shoppers are individuals who meet superb income and internet genuinely really really worth requirements and are taken into consideration to be extremely-present day investors. Because non-public REITs aren't publicly traded, they'll be normally plenty much less liquid than public REITs, this means that that buyers may also additionally moreover have a greater tough time selling their shares in the event that they need to liquidate their investment.

However, personal REITs can also provide a few benefits to buyers. For instance, due to the fact non-public REITs aren't problem to the identical regulatory necessities as public REITs, they'll have greater flexibility in their funding strategies. Additionally, personal REITs may be able to offer better returns to buyers than public REITs, because of the truth they do no longer need to pay the prices associated with being publicly traded.

Overall, whether or no longer to spend money on a public or personal REIT will rely upon hundreds of of factors, which includes an investor's investment dreams, hazard tolerance, and liquidity needs. Public REITs have a tendency to offer more liquidity and extra transparency, on the identical time as non-public REITs can also offer more flexibility and probable better returns. Investors need to carefully remember the risks and advantages of each public and private REITs before making any funding selections.

Investing in individual REITs

Investing in individual Real Estate Investment Trusts (REITs) may be a manner for purchasers to benefit publicity to specific actual belongings assets or sectors. By making an funding in individual REITs, customers can doubtlessly benefit from the profits-producing capability and functionality for capital appreciation of a specific belongings type or market sector.

One advantage of creating an funding in man or woman REITs is that customers can select out the unique REITs they need to put money into primarily based on their funding desires and risk tolerance. For instance, traders who are interested by profits-generating investments may additionally additionally pick out to invest in fairness REITs that focus on houses collectively with apartment houses or buying facilities. Investors who are interested in real estate debt might also additionally pick out to put money into mortgage REITs that target residential or commercial enterprise mortgages.

However, making an investment in character REITs also can have some drawbacks. One capability chance is that making an investment in character REITs can cause a lack of diversification. If an investor handiest invests in a single REIT or a few REITs, they'll be mission to the precise dangers related to the ones REITs. For example, if an investor excellent invests in equity REITs that focus on a single market area, which include healthcare or retail, they'll be state of affairs to the dangers related to that location, which include adjustments in consumer conduct or regulatory modifications.

Another capacity hazard of creating an funding in character REITs is that the general overall performance of a specific REIT can be stricken by elements which can be out of doors of the investor's manage. For instance, if a REIT owns homes which might be located in a geographic area that studies natural screw ups or economic downturns, the fee of the REIT's shares may additionally additionally moreover decline.

Overall, making an investment in character REITs can be a manner for customers to advantage exposure to unique actual belongings property or sectors. However, shoppers need to cautiously take into account the risks and advantages of making an funding in character REITs, similarly to their personal funding dreams and risk tolerance, earlier than making any investment picks.

Additionally, buyers might also moreover furthermore need to remember diversifying their real belongings investments by using making an funding in a aggregate of individual REITs, REIT change-traded price range (ETFs), or distinct real property funding options.

Investing in REIT mutual price variety or change-traded rate range (ETFs)

Investing in Real Estate Investment Trust (REIT) mutual rate range or exchange-traded charge range (ETFs) can be a manner for shoppers to gain publicity to a diverse portfolio of REITs. These rate variety invest in a number of REITs, that could assist to mitigate a number of the dangers related to making an investment in character REITs.

REIT mutual price range and ETFs provide shoppers a number of benefits. One gain is that they provide a high degree of diversification. Because those funds spend money on an entire lot of REITs, they're able to assist to unfold hazard throughout extremely good belongings sorts and geographic locations. This can potentially lessen the impact of any single REIT's terrible regular performance on the overall portfolio.

Another benefit of making an funding in REIT mutual budget or ETFs is that they're commonly more liquid than individual REITs. Because the ones price range are traded on a public alternate, investors can without problems buy and sell stocks, making it less complicated to alter their funding portfolio as market situations change.

In addition, REIT mutual fee variety and ETFs can be more less expensive for a few customers than making an investment in individual REITs. Because the ones rate range invest in severa REITs, the minimal funding required to benefit publicity to a varied REIT portfolio may be lower than the minimum funding required to shop for individual REIT shares.

However, there are also some functionality drawbacks to creating an funding in REIT mutual finances and ETFs. One functionality drawback is that the ones finances might also have control prices, which could erode some of the returns generated through manner of the underlying REITs. Additionally, those price range can be trouble to marketplace risk, interest price chance, and specific dangers associated with making an funding in real belongings assets.

Overall, making an investment in REIT mutual fee variety or ETFs may be a manner for buyers to benefit publicity to a numerous portfolio of REITs. These fee variety offer a number of benefits, collectively with diversification, liquidity, and affordability. However, consumers must carefully remember the dangers and fees related to investing in the ones budget before making any funding selections. Additionally, buyers also can need to speak over with a financial guide to determine if making an investment in REIT mutual charge range or ETFs is appropriate for their man or woman investment goals and chance tolerance.

Chapter 10: Considerations For Making

Investing in Real Estate Investment Trusts (REITs) may be a way for buyers to advantage publicity to the real assets market, in all likelihood generating profits and capital appreciation. However, earlier than making an funding in REITs, there are numerous troubles that shoppers must consider.

One critical consideration is the shape of REIT wherein the investor is involved. As cited earlier, there are numerous sorts of REITs, collectively with fairness REITs, mortgage REITs, and hybrid REITs. Each form of REIT has remarkable funding tendencies and risks, and clients need to cautiously recollect which type of REIT is suitable for their funding dreams and threat tolerance.

Another hobby is the general overall performance of the underlying real estate belongings. REITs are brilliant as sturdy due to the fact the homes in which they make investments, so clients need to carefully observe the awesome and simple performance of the houses held through the usage of a given REIT. Factors to consider may also include occupancy fees, condo charges, upkeep and repair charges, and close by market conditions.

Investors ought to additionally test the manage group of the REIT they are thinking about making an investment in. The excellent and revel in of the management crew can also have a huge impact at the fulfillment of the REIT. Investors might also moreover want to research the track record of the REIT's control group and take a look at their enjoy and qualifications.

Another critical interest for investing in REITs is prices. REITs can be problem to manipulate fees, that would erode a number of the returns generated with the aid of the use of the underlying actual belongings belongings. Investors want to cautiously evaluation the costs related to a given REIT earlier than making any investment alternatives.

Finally, investors ought to cautiously compare their very private funding goals and risk tolerance before investing in REITs. Like any funding, investing in REITs carries some degree of threat, and consumers need to only spend money on REITs which may be suitable for his or her individual funding goals and danger tolerance. Investors may additionally moreover need to visit a financial representative to assist them examine their funding goals and decide which REITs are suitable for his or her man or woman goals.

Key economic metrics to assess

When comparing Real Estate Investment Trusts (REITs) as capability investments, there are various key financial metrics that customers want to take into account. These metrics can help investors look at the monetary fitness and basic overall performance of a given REIT, and make knowledgeable funding picks.

One critical economic metric to remember is rate range from operations (FFO). FFO is a measure of a REIT's cash waft, and is calculated with the useful resource of manner of consisting of depreciation and amortization costs to internet profits. Because REITs are required to pay out at the least ninety% of their taxable earnings as dividends to shareholders, FFO can help shoppers take a look at the REIT's capability to generate income to beneficial aid dividend payments.

Another key financial metric to undergo in thoughts is net asset charge (NAV). NAV is a measure of a REIT's underlying asset rate, and is calculated thru subtracting the REIT's liabilities from the fee of its belongings. Investors can use NAV to assess whether or not or now not or no longer a given REIT is shopping for and selling at a reduction or premium to its underlying asset rate.

Dividend yield is each different essential economic metric for comparing REITs. Dividend yield is calculated with the useful resource of dividing the as soon as a twelve months dividend payout via manner of the modern-day stock charge. This metric can assist investors look at the earnings-producing capability of a given REIT, and study the REIT's dividend yield to exceptional income-producing investments.

Debt-to-equity ratio is some other key financial metric to take into account while comparing REITs. This metric compares a REIT's debt to its equity, and can assist shoppers look at the REIT's leverage and financial fitness. A immoderate debt-to-equity ratio may additionally additionally endorse that a REIT is incredibly leveraged and can be extra vulnerable to modifications in hobby charges or other financial factors.

Finally, buyers may additionally additionally need to bear in mind the fee-to-profits (P/E) ratio when comparing REITs. P/E ratio compares a REIT's stock charge to its income consistent with percentage, and might help buyers study whether or not a given REIT is buying and selling at a top elegance or good buy to its profits functionality.

Overall, there are numerous key monetary metrics that buyers have to do not forget on the equal time as evaluating Real Estate Investment Trusts (REITs) as potential investments. These metrics can help customers compare the monetary fitness and overall performance of a given REIT, and make informed investment choices. However, customers have to additionally do not forget one-of-a-type factors, collectively with the quality of the underlying real property belongings and the control institution, earlier than making any funding alternatives.

Understanding the real belongings marketplace and the manner it influences REITs

Real Estate Investment Trusts (REITs) are immediately tied to the actual belongings marketplace, and changes inside the actual property marketplace may additionally have a massive effect at the overall performance of REITs. As such, knowledge the actual estate market is crucial for investors who are thinking about making an investment in REITs.

One hassle that would have an effect on the real estate market and, in flip, REITs, is hobby costs. When interest prices are low, it could be less complex and additional low priced for buyers to borrow coins to shop for real belongings property. This can bring about prolonged call for for real property and likely higher assets values. On the opportunity hand, even as hobby fees are immoderate, borrowing costs may moreover growth, that could lessen call for for real property and probably lower property values. Changes in interest prices also can have an effect at the price of borrowing for REITs, that might impact their profitability.

Another detail which can have an impact on the real assets marketplace and REITs is the overall monetary climate. When the economic device is strong and unemployment is low, clients also can have greater disposable earnings to spend on real belongings, that could reason extended call for and doubtlessly higher property values. Conversely, while the financial device is inclined and unemployment is excessive, clients can also have much less disposable income to spend on actual assets, that could lessen name for and potentially lower assets values. Changes within the financial climate also can have an effect on the apartment expenses that REITs can fee for their residences, which can effect their profits and profitability.

Real belongings marketplace situations can also range via using vicinity and property kind. For instance, positive geographic regions also can enjoy extra population growth or more potent financial growth than others, that may motive prolonged call for for real property in the ones regions. Similarly, positive belongings types, which includes residences or healthcare facilities, may additionally additionally revel in higher call for than others, that may effect the overall overall performance of REITs that specialize within the ones belongings sorts.

Overall, knowledge the real property market is crucial for investors who are considering making an funding in REITs. Changes in interest charges, the general monetary climate, and geographic and assets type-particular market situations can all have a sizable impact on the overall typical performance of REITs. By staying knowledgeable approximately those elements, shoppers can make greater knowledgeable funding options and in all likelihood mitigate a number of the dangers related to making an funding in REITs.

Chapter 11: Risks Associated With Making An Investment In Reits

Real Estate Investment Trusts (REITs) can be a in all likelihood attractive funding for buyers searching for exposure to the real property marketplace. However, as with every investment, there are also risks related to making an funding in REITs that customers have to be privy to.

One capability risk of investing in REITs is the capability for modifications in interest fees. REITs usually deliver a significant amount of debt, which may be impacted with the aid of way of modifications in interest prices. If interest prices upward push, the charge of borrowing for REITs may growth, that might reduce their profitability and possibly cause declines in their percent prices.

Another capability threat of investing in REITs is that they may be problem to the identical dangers as different real belongings investments, which includes adjustments in property values and apartment expenses.

REITs can be impacted via adjustments inside the real assets market, that may effect their potential to generate profits and probably motive declines in their percent costs.

Additionally, some REITs may be extra at risk of terrific risks than others. For instance, REITs focusing on a particular property kind, together with healthcare centers or buying facilities, can be more liable to changes in purchaser conduct or regulatory adjustments that impact that assets kind.

REITs also can be trouble to liquidity threat. While REITs are usually greater liquid than individual actual estate investments, they will though be hassle to liquidity risk if there are restrained purchasers or sellers of their shares. This must make it greater hard for clients to shop for or sell stocks of the REIT, potentially impacting the fee of their investment.

Finally, it's miles important for customers to cautiously examine the manipulate organisation of the REIT they are considering making an investment in. Poor control decisions can bring about declines inside the rate of the REIT and likely effect its capability to generate income.

Overall, making an investment in REITs consists of some degree of risk. Investors need to cautiously evaluate the dangers and advantages of making an investment in REITs, and do not forget diversifying their actual property investments in some unspecified time in the future of exquisite belongings types and geographic places to mitigate some of the risks related to any unmarried investment. Additionally, traders might also moreover want to talk over with a monetary marketing consultant to decide whether or not investing in REITs is appropriate for their individual investment desires and threat tolerance.

REITs and taxes

Real Estate Investment Trusts (REITs) are required via law to distribute as a minimum ninety% of their taxable earnings to their shareholders as dividends. This makes REITs an attractive investment for investors seeking out regular profits, as the dividends paid by way of the usage of REITs are normally better than those paid via unique shares.

However, buyers need to additionally be aware about the tax implications of creating an investment in REITs. Because REITs are required to distribute a massive aspect in their earnings to shareholders, their dividends are normally taxed at a higher fee than wonderful sorts of dividend-paying stocks. This is due to the fact REIT dividends are generally handled as ordinary profits, in desire to as licensed dividends, which may be situation to decrease tax costs.

In addition, some of the profits generated with the aid of REITs may be assignment to nonresident withholding taxes. This can impact buyers who are not residents of the u . S . In which the REIT is domiciled. Investors need to cautiously assessment the tax implications of making an investment in REITs

160

of their home united states of america and the usa of the united states wherein the REIT is domiciled to ensure that they're privy to any functionality tax liabilities.

Another important tax attention for REIT buyers is the capacity for double taxation. Because REITs are required to distribute a huge thing of their income to shareholders, they'll be task to a lower diploma of business enterprise taxation than extraordinary varieties of groups. However, because of the reality REIT dividends are generally dealt with as normal income, they will be project to double taxation at the shareholder diploma. This technique that the earnings generated by way of the usage of manner of the REIT is taxed on the corporation level, and as a substitute on the equal time as it's miles disbursed to shareholders as dividends.

Finally, it's miles vital for purchasers to be aware of the capability for nation and neighborhood taxes whilst making an funding in REITs. Different states may additionally

additionally moreover have unique tax guidelines for REITs, and consumers want to carefully examine the tax implications of making an investment in REITs of their domestic kingdom.

Overall, making an investment in REITs should have tax implications that customers should be aware of. While REITs can be an attractive investment for earnings-looking for traders, the ability for higher taxes and double taxation want to be carefully taken into consideration. Investors can also moreover need to visit a tax professional or financial advertising and marketing consultant to determine the tax implications of creating an investment in REITs and to boom a tax-green funding approach.

Tax blessings of making an funding in REITs

Real Estate Investment Trusts (REITs) offer severa tax advantages that could cause them to an appealing investment for notable traders.

One key tax gain of investing in REITs is that they are required to distribute at least 90% in their taxable earnings to shareholders as dividends. This technique that REITs do not pay federal earnings tax at the profits that they distribute to their shareholders. As a cease result, REIT dividends are normally taxed on the shareholder degree, rather than on the company diploma, that may bring about a decrease everyday tax burden for consumers.

Another potential tax gain of making an investment in REITs is that they'll be eligible for the 20% pass-via deduction for licensed organisation profits. This deduction, which have become brought as part of the Tax Cuts and Jobs Act of 2017, lets in satisfactory companies, alongside facet REITs, to deduct up to twenty% of their certified enterprise income from their taxable earnings. This deduction can extensively lessen the tax jail responsibility for buyers who maintain REIT shares in taxable payments.

Additionally, because of the reality REITs are required to distribute a excellent element in their earnings to shareholders, they'll be less in all likelihood to build up undistributed earnings that might be problem to double taxation. This way that REIT buyers may be much less likely to face double taxation on the company and shareholder degree, as is the case with different sorts of organizations.

Finally, sure styles of REITs may be eligible for special tax remedy. For instance, timber REITs can be eligible for the particular tax remedy that applies to wooded place and agricultural assets. This remedy can bring about lower taxes for customers who hold shares in wood REITs.

Overall, making an funding in REITs can provide severa tax advantages that would reason them to an attractive funding for high-quality customers. However, it's miles important for investors to cautiously assessment the tax implications of making an investment in REITs in their individual situations, and to are seeking recommendation from a tax professional or monetary manual to enlarge a tax-green funding technique.

Chapter 12: Particular Degrees Of The Real Property Market Cycle

Real Estate Investment Trusts (REITs) can carry out in every other manner in unique degrees of the actual property market cycle. The actual property market cycle is typically divided into 4 degrees: boom, hypersupply, recession, and healing. Understanding how REITs carry out in every level of the cycle can assist buyers make extra knowledgeable funding alternatives.

During the growth degree, the real assets market is typically experiencing boom and growing name for for houses. This can be an notable environment for REITs, as they will be able to gain from developing property values and rental expenses. During this stage, investors also can want to bear in mind making an investment in REITs focusing on belongings kinds which can be in immoderate call for, collectively with residential or place of business houses.

During the hypersupply diploma, the actual belongings market may be experiencing an oversupply of homes, that may bring about declining belongings values and rental charges. This may be a hard environment for REITs, as their income and profitability may be impacted via decrease condo charges and progressed opposition. During this stage, consumers also can moreover need to be more cautious while making an investment in REITs, and may want to keep in mind making an investment in REITs that specialize in property kinds that are an entire lot a lot less impacted with the aid of oversupply, which encompass healthcare centers or self-storage homes.

During the recession diploma, the actual assets market is generally experiencing a decline in call for for homes and declining assets values. This can be a hard surroundings for REITs, as they will be impacted with the resource of lower condominium prices and decreased occupancy ranges. However, a few REITs can be higher positioned to climate a recession, inclusive of these that target important offerings or people with sturdy stability sheets. Investors may also moreover want to do not forget making an funding in the ones sorts of REITs all through this degree of the cycle.

During the recuperation diploma, the real property market is typically experiencing a go back to growth and developing call for for homes. This can be a outstanding environment for REITs, as they'll be capable of gain from growing property values and condominium expenses. During this diploma, purchasers may additionally moreover need to remember making an investment in REITs focusing on property kinds which might be predicted to revel in sturdy name for, which includes logistics or statistics middle houses.

Overall, REITs can perform in a considered one of a type way in one in all a kind levels of the actual estate marketplace cycle. Investors ought to carefully take a look at the underlying basics of the real property marketplace and the precise REITs they may be considering making an funding in to decide whether or not or not they will be nicely-located to perform in a given diploma of the cycle. Additionally, buyers may also additionally want to consider diversifying their real estate investments for the duration of high-quality assets kinds and geographic locations to mitigate a number of the dangers associated with any unmarried investment.

Strategies for making an funding in REITs in some unspecified time in the future of specific marketplace cycles

Real Estate Investment Trusts (REITs) can perform in a different way in one in all a type tiers of the actual belongings marketplace cycle. As such, investors can also want to remember unique strategies for making an investment in REITs throughout special marketplace cycles.

During the increase diploma of the actual property market cycle, clients also can need to don't forget making an investment in REITs focusing on assets types which can be predicted to experience sturdy call for, which includes residential or office houses. Additionally, customers may additionally moreover need to recollect making an investment in REITs that have strong balance sheets and a song document of constant income and dividend increase. Diversifying across terrific assets kinds and geographic locations also can assist to mitigate a number of the dangers related to any unmarried funding.

During the hypersupply diploma, consumers also can additionally want to be extra careful while making an investment in REITs, and can want to preserve in thoughts making an funding in REITs focusing on property types which can be a extraordinary deal tons much less impacted with the beneficial useful resource of oversupply, which consist of healthcare centers or self-storage houses. Additionally, traders may additionally need to search for REITs with robust tenant relationships and prolonged-time period leases, as the ones can assist to provide greater strong income streams at some stage in a tough market surroundings.

During the recession degree, traders also can want to take into account making an investment in protective REITs focusing on essential offerings, including healthcare centers or grocery-anchored retail facilities. Additionally, investors may also additionally want to look for REITs with robust balance sheets and get proper of get entry to to to capital, as those can assist to weather a downturn and feature the REIT for capability increase inside the future.

During the healing degree, buyers can also moreover need to recall making an investment in REITs specializing in belongings kinds which may be predicted to experience sturdy call for, together with logistics or records center houses. Additionally, investors may want to look for REITs that have a song document of constant earnings and dividend boom, as the ones can provide extra reliable earnings streams in some unspecified time in the future of a marketplace upswing.

Overall, making an funding in REITs sooner or later of particular stages of the real belongings marketplace cycle requires careful assessment of marketplace conditions and the underlying basics of the REITs being taken into consideration. Diversifying throughout super assets kinds and geographic places can also help to mitigate a number of the risks related to any unmarried funding. Additionally, investors may additionally need to visit a economic guide to expand a well-numerous and market-responsive investment approach.

Chapter 13: Examples Of Fulfillment Reit Investments

Real Estate Investment Trusts (REITs) can offer consumers with the opportunity to spend money on real belongings without the want to buy bodily houses. While there can be no guarantee of achievement on the same time as making an investment in REITs, there have been numerous examples of a achievement REIT investments over the years.

One example of a a achievement REIT funding is Simon Property Group (SPG). SPG is the maximum critical mall REIT in the United States and has a track file of normal profits and dividend boom. Despite worrying conditions going via the retail enterprise in cutting-edge years, SPG has been able to hold robust occupancy rates and growth its earnings and dividends through the years. As of 2021, SPG is extensively considered to be one of the most a success REIT investments of all time.

Another example of a a success REIT funding is Prologis (PLD), a international logistics REIT that specializes within the possession and manage of business business enterprise houses. PLD has benefited from the boom of e-trade and the extended call for for warehouse and distribution facilities. In latest years, PLD has improved its operations globally and has a track file of constant earnings and dividend boom.

Digital Realty Trust (DLR) is every other example of a a fulfillment REIT funding. DLR is a worldwide facts middle REIT that specializes inside the ownership and manage of residences which might be vital to the operation of statistics centers and cloud computing. DLR has benefited from the stepped forward name for for data garage and processing, and has a track report of normal income and dividend boom.

Overall, a fulfillment REIT investments have a tendency to be those which can be properly-numerous during one of a type belongings kinds and geographic locations, have sturdy management organizations, and characteristic a tune file of consistent income and dividend boom. While beyond average general performance isn't any guarantee of destiny success, investors can use the records of successful REIT investments to help inform their investment alternatives and take a look at the capability of REITs they'll be thinking about making an funding in. It is crucial to have a look at that investing in REITs consists of dangers, and buyers must cautiously evaluate the risks and benefits of making an funding in any person REIT.

Lessons observed out from the ones investments

The achievement reminiscences of Real Estate Investment Trust (REIT) investments inclusive of Simon Property Group, Prologis, and Digital Realty Trust can provide treasured instructions for buyers.

One key lesson that may be determined from those a fulfillment REIT investments is the importance of diversification. Each of these REITs has a severa portfolio of houses at some point of unique geographic locations and belongings kinds. This diversification facilitates to reduce the threat of any single assets or geographic vicinity having a big effect on the general ordinary overall performance of the REIT.

Another lesson that can be discovered from those a success REIT investments is the significance of a robust manage institution. All 3 of these REITs have skilled and effective manipulate groups which have been able to navigate through hard market situations and capitalize on opportunities for boom.

A 1/3 lesson that can be decided from those successful REIT investments is the importance of identifying prolonged-term trends and opportunities. For example, Prologis has been able to revel in the boom of e-alternate and the advanced name for for warehouse and distribution facilities. Similarly, Digital Realty

Trust has been able to enjoy the advanced call for for information garage and processing.

Finally, the ones a fulfillment REIT investments spotlight the significance of regular income and dividend growth. Each of these REITs has a tune record of normal earnings and dividend boom, which has helped to draw and hold shoppers over the long term.

Overall, the success reminiscences of those REIT investments can offer precious commands for buyers. Diversification, robust manipulate, identifying long-time period tendencies, and regular profits and dividend increase are all essential factors to bear in mind whilst comparing REIT investments. While beyond standard performance isn't any guarantee of future fulfillment, shoppers can use the ones instructions to tell their funding selections and possibly growth their opportunities of achievement even as investing in REITs.

Chapter 14: Potential Growth Of The Reit Enterprise

The Real Estate Investment Trust (REIT) enterprise has skilled huge boom at some point of the previous few a few years, and there may be capacity for continued boom inside the future.

One key element the use of the boom of the REIT industry is the developing name for for real property investments from institutional and man or woman investors. As interest costs have remained low and stock market volatility has improved, many traders have grew to emerge as to real belongings as an opportunity funding choice. REITs offer shoppers with a manner to spend money on actual belongings with out the want for direct belongings ownership, and can offer diversification, liquidity, and doubtlessly attractive returns.

Another detail using the boom of the REIT employer is the developing availability of worldwide investment opportunities. Many

REITs have expanded their operations internationally, offering buyers with exposure to a greater variety of geographic locations and assets kinds. As the global real assets market continues to expand, REITs can be well-located to benefit from this growth.

Additionally, the upward thrust of era and records analytics is anticipated to have a considerable impact on the REIT organisation. As REITs come to be greater current-day in their use of generation and information, they will be capable of end up conscious of recent investment opportunities and optimize their portfolios for max returns.

Finally, regulatory adjustments might also additionally make contributions to the increase of the REIT business agency. For example, the modern increase of the definition of a REIT inside the United States to encompass renewable electricity initiatives may also additionally cause extended funding on this place.

Overall, the REIT organization has expert vast growth in some unspecified time in the future of the last few a few years, and there can be ability for continued boom inside the destiny. Factors which incorporates growing demand from buyers, international investment opportunities, technology and statistics analytics, and regulatory changes may moreover moreover all make contributions to this boom. While the destiny is constantly unsure, the REIT agency might also offer appealing funding possibilities for the ones seeking to diversify their portfolios and invest in real belongings.

Trends to examine within the REIT market

The Real Estate Investment Trust (REIT) marketplace is continuously evolving, and there are several traits to have a examine that can have a extensive effect on the business enterprise.

One fashion to look at is the upward thrust of environmental, social, and governance (ESG) making an investment. ESG making an funding specializes in organizations that prioritize environmental sustainability, social obligation, and pinnacle governance practices. Many REITs have already taken steps to prioritize ESG elements of their operations, along with reducing carbon emissions or improving strength universal overall performance in their homes. As ESG making an funding continues to benefit popularity, REITs that prioritize ESG elements can be properly-placed to draw funding and outperform those that don't.

Another style to take a look at is the growing use of technology and facts analytics within the REIT industry. As REITs end up more state-of-the-art in their use of era and information, they may be better equipped to pick out out new funding opportunities, optimize their portfolios for maximum returns, and beautify tenant reminiscences. For example, some REITs are the usage of records analytics to investigate tenant behavior and options, and the use of this records to make improvements to their homes and offerings.

A 0.33 fashion to have a look at is the developing name for for alternative belongings types, including senior housing, self-garage centers, and facts centers. As technology maintains to reshape the economic machine, there can be extended call for for houses that cater to new industries and organisation models. REITs focusing on the ones kinds of homes can be nicely-placed to gain from this fashion.

Finally, adjustments in hobby costs and monetary situations can also have a massive impact at the REIT market. Rising hobby costs may also make borrowing greater costly for REITs, that might impact their functionality to accumulate new houses or make improvements to modern homes. Additionally, monetary downturns may also motive declining property values and reduce occupancy expenses, which could effect the earnings and profitability of REITs.

Overall, the REIT market is constantly evolving, and there are various traits to have a study which can have a big impact on the company. Investors ought to live informed about those developments and don't forget how they will effect the overall performance of man or woman REITs and the company as a whole.

Summary of key factors

Real Estate Investment Trusts (REITs) are funding automobiles that permit shoppers to invest in actual assets with out the need for direct belongings ownership. Some of the key points to recognize about REITs encompass:

REITs can provide diversification advantages, get proper of access to to actual property without proudly proudly owning assets, potential for high dividends, and functionality for capital appreciation.

There are 3 critical kinds of REITs: equity REITs, mortgage REITs, and hybrid REITs.

Investors can put money into individual REITs, REIT mutual funds, or exchange-traded price range (ETFs) that keep portfolios of REITs.

Some of the important thing economic metrics to don't forget at the same time as evaluating REITs encompass budget from operations (FFO), net asset fee (NAV), and dividend yield.

Understanding the real property marketplace and the manner it influences REITs is important for making informed investment decisions.

Some of the dangers related to investing in REITs encompass hobby price risk, market threat, and liquidity chance.

REITs may provide tax benefits for customers, including the ability to pass thru income to buyers and avoid double taxation.